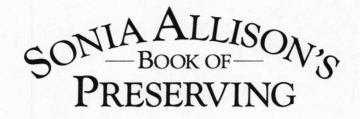

SONIA ALLISON'S
—BOOK OF—
PRESERVING

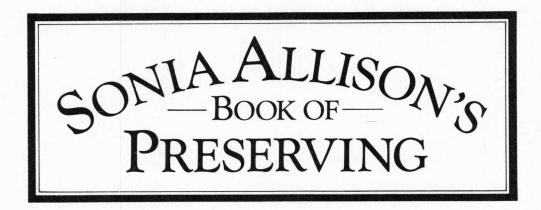

SONIA ALLISON'S
—BOOK OF—
PRESERVING

DAVID & CHARLES

NEWTON ABBOT LONDON

NORTH POMFRET (Vt)

Drawings by Andrew Harrison
Colour print courtesy of Beaches of Salisbury

British Library Cataloguing in Publication Data

Allison, Sonia
    Sonia Allison's book of practical preserving.
    1. Food – Preservation – Amateur's manuals
    I. Book of practical preserving
    641.4   TX601

    ISBN 0–7153–7817–1

Library of Congress Catalog Card Number
79–51085

© Sonia Allison, 1979

Typeset by Ronset Ltd, Darwen, Lancashire
and printed in Great Britain
by Redwood Burn Ltd, Tonbridge
for David & Charles (Publishers) Limited
Brunel House   Newton Abbot   Devon

Published in the United States of America
by David & Charles Inc
North Pomfret   Vermont 05053   USA

Contents

PART I
Methods

PART II
A-Z of Fruits and Vegetables

PART I
Methods
Introduction

Practical preserving to me means never by-passing fruit and vegetables on 'special offer' at local shops and markets, cashing-in on gluts and using up home-grown produce in the most advantageous and economical ways.

For these reasons, this book has been planned with 'master' methods and basic recipes at the front, followed by an alphabetical list of crops for quick and easy reference. Thus, if you have a wealth of beans and want to salt or freeze them, or are knee-deep in garden windfalls and fancy apple chutney, you simply read the appropriate chapters on salting, freezing and chutney-making *first*, and *then* follow the individual entries for proportions, variations and different-from-usual combinations.

I have concentrated on bottling, chutney-making, drying, freezing and making fruit cheeses, butters, curds, purées and syrups. In addition, there are recipes and methods covering jams, jellies, marmalades and mincemeat, as well as instructions for pickling, salting and making sauces or ketchups. Luxury touches will be found in the form of fruits in alcohol and candied peel.

This book has been deliberately geared for others such as myself – busy people with more enthusiasm than spare time!

The 'granny receipts' included at the ends of the chapters in Part 1 come from old cookery books that have given me hours of pleasure, and much insight into how things used to be done. Techniques have obviously changed since these were written. Our ancestors worked by feel, and were sometimes remarkably successful; but they used rule-of-thumb measurements and had a blissful disregard for temperatures, caution and even hygiene. I hope you will share my enjoyment of reading these old-time ideas.

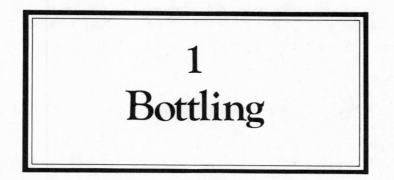

1
Bottling

Frozen fruits sit unseen and unpretentiously in the freezer gathering ice: preserving in modern times. Bottled fruits, spread out on larder shelves, are a splendid sight for all to see, and a colourful display of jars, with neatly written labels describing the contents, gives one immense personal satisfaction and pride. This probably explains the continued interest in fruit-bottling; freezing is simpler, easier and less complicated, yet bottling is as popular as it ever was and is undertaken with dedication and care year after year by enthusiasts of all ages.

Those unfamiliar with bottling will need to read this section through carefully. Old hands may regard it as something of a refresher course.

There are several methods of bottling from which to choose, but here I must emphasise that these methods apply *only* to fruits and tomatoes, and *never* should vegetables, meat or fish be bottled. The result could prove fatal and these items need to be preserved by expert technicians in factory conditions.

How Bottling Works

Bottling works by sterilising the contents of every jar so that the fruit remains in sound condition, with no deterioration, for at least one year. For effective sterilisation, the fruit must be adequately heated (this will be explained later) in undamaged preserving jars, and the lids must form an airtight seal so that when the contents of the jars are completely cold, the vacuum formed within will hold the lids securely in place. One of the standard tests to see if the processing has worked properly is to lift up each jar, when cold, by the lid. If the lid stays put, all is well and the fruit has been satisfactorily sterilised. If the lid comes off, the fruit must

be reprocessed or, alternatively, treated as freshly cooked fruit and used up fairly speedily.

Equipment

Basically, equipment for fruit bottling is undemanding. The main items necessary are preserving jars with matching lids, and rubber rings which fit snugly underneath. Some of the newer jars have lids with built-in rubber rings, so check this out before buying separate rings.

There are two main kinds of fastenings that go with the preserving jars. The most common are metal screw bands which are fitted *loosely* to the jars during processing in order to allow air and steam to escape and prevent the jars from bursting. (The exception here is for the oven methods of processing, explained later.) After processing, the bands are screwed on to the jars as tightly as possible so that the lids are held securely in place until the contents have cooled and a vacuum formed. If the insides of the screw bands are brushed lightly with a little salad oil they will turn more easily.

The other type of 'fastening' is the spring-clip variety which holds the lid firmly in position during processing. As the contents of the jar become hot, the clip allows the lid to lift up slightly, enabling air and steam to escape. As the jar cools down, and a vacuum forms inside it, the clip grips the lid tightly.

Most good hardware and kitchenware shops stock a wide selection of preserving jars and you will probably need some of each size so that you can bottle large or small quantities according to the amount of fruit available. When buying new or unfamiliar jars, make sure you have the relevant instructions.

There are four important things to note in relation to equipment:

1 To make the rubber bands pliable so that they fit properly, they should be soaked for about a quarter of an hour in very hot water immediately before use. The bands should be used *once* only so you have to buy new ones each time you undertake bottling.

2 Lids with built-in rubber bands should *never* be used more than once. To check if a lid of this type has formed an effective seal, make sure its centre portion has been sucked downwards when cold. This will show as a shallow depression and indicate that the processing has been carried out satisfactorily.

3 Glass jars with chips round the neck or rim should *not* be used. Nor should chipped glass lids because the seal will be poor and contamination of the contents will quickly result.

4 Just before use, all jars and lids must be well washed, rinsed under hot running water and left to drain, upside-down, on a surface lined with a clean, dry tea-towel. Do not wipe the jars but shake off surplus water if necessary.

Bottling Liquids

Fruit may be bottled either in water only, a method ideal for diabetics and those on low-sugar diets, or in syrup, which enhances the appearance, colour and flavour of the fruit. The average basic proportion is 225g (8oz) granulated or cube sugar to 575ml (1pt) water, but the sugar can be decreased or increased according to the sharpness of the fruit. The denser the syrup (in other words, the more sugar to water) the more likelihood there is of the fruit rising in the jars. This matters not a jot for home use but is obviously unsatisfactory for competitions.

Therefore if you are exhibiting bottles of fruit, the proportion of sugar to water should be reduced to about 125–175g (4–6oz) to every 575ml (1pt).

To make syrup, dissolve sugar in water, over low heat, stirring. Boil briskly for one minute. Use hot or cold as specified under individual entries. It may be useful to know that 225g (8oz) sugar to 575ml (1pt) water is sufficient for about $4 \times \frac{1}{2}$kg (1lb) jars or 2×1kg (2lb) jars.

Choosing and Preparing Fruit

All fruit for bottling must be in sound condition. It should be *just* ripe, as fresh as possible and unblemished. Bruised or marked fruits are best used for other purposes.

Rinse fruit gently under plenty of cold, running water (but not raspberries which damage so easily), then prepare it as if it were going to be stewed. For example, cut rhubarb into $2\frac{1}{2}$cm (1in) lengths; top and tail gooseberries and nick each one to stop shrivelling; take currants off stalks; hull berry fruits; halve plums and remove stones; skin peaches by blanching as tomatoes, then halve and remove stones. Process quickly to prevent colour spoilage.

To slow down the browning of apples and pears, make up a light brine by dissolving 25g (1oz) salt in about $2\frac{1}{2}$ litres (4pt) cold water. Peel and core fruit and slice it directly into the salted water. Pack into jars straight from the brine, rinse thoroughly by filling jars with cold water and then tipping it away, and finally process as specified under individual entries.

Packing the Fruit into Jars

Where possible, grade fruit according to

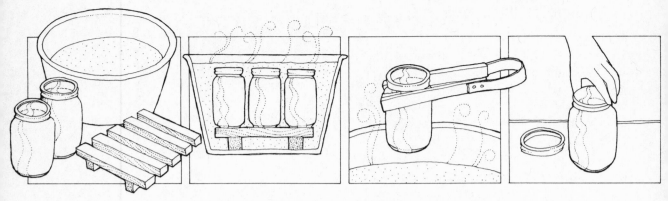

size, shape, sharpness (or sweetness) and ripeness. Pack tightly into jars, taking care not to bruise the fruit by dropping it in from a height. Use the handle of a wooden spoon to ease the pieces of fruit into place, then shake down by gently tapping the base of each jar against a thick, folded towel. Fill with hot or cold water or syrup either before or after processing. Be guided in this by individual entries.

Special Note: Tomatoes and Strawberries

Tomatoes, if small, should be bottled whole. Pack into jars then cover to the brim with brine made by dissolving 15 g (½oz) salt in 1¼ litres (2pt) water. Also add ¼ level teaspoon citric acid or 2 teaspoons lemon juice to the contents of every ½kg (1lb) jar. For 'solid pack' tomatoes, blanch medium fruits, remove skins, then cut into eighths. Gently toss every 1½kg (3lb) with 1½ tablespoons lemon juice, 1½ level teaspoons salt and 1½ level teaspoons caster sugar. Pack well down into warm preserving jar (or jars) and process as directed.

If preferred, add ¾ level teaspoon citric acid instead of lemon juice but *do not* omit acid altogether, otherwise the safety of the tomatoes will be in jeopardy.

Strawberries become pallid and shrunken unless treated as follows:
Hull fruit. Put into bowl. Cover with boiling syrup tinted deep red with food colouring. Leave overnight. Pack into jars and process as directed under individual entries.

Methods of Bottling

Method 1 Slow water bath: jars filled with cold water or syrup; preserving thermometer required

This is a method of processing carried out on top of the cooker; in a fish kettle if you have one, in an old-fashioned preserving pan which is broad-based and deep (certainly deep enough for the jars to be completely immersed in the water), or in a very large saucepan or even a clean pail. What is essential is a false bottom, to stop the jars coming into direct contact with the base of the pan; this can be a small metal grill pan or saucepan rack, some slats of wood nailed together in a criss-cross fashion, or even several thicknesses of sacking; anything, in fact, which will raise the jars.

To prepare, fill the bottles of packed fruit with cold water or cold syrup, then fit on rubber rings, lids, clips and/or screw bands. If using screw bands, tighten fully then

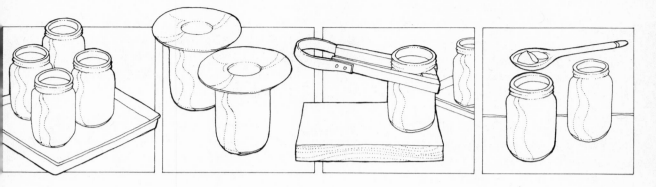

loosen by a quarter-turn to allow air and steam to escape (see previous notes in this section under 'How Bottling Works' and 'Equipment'). Place jars in the pan etc, making sure they are completely covered with *cold* water but *not* knocking against each other.

Over a period of 1½ hours, bring the water to the temperature given under individual entries, checking frequently with a thermometer especially designed for preservation. *Do not use a medical thermometer*. Maintain the temperature for the length of time specified (again note individual entries) which can vary from 10 minutes (gooseberries) to 40 minutes ('solid pack' tomatoes).

When processing is complete, carefully remove jars from pan using either tongs or a hand protected with a thick oven glove. Stand the jars on a wooden board or working surface covered with a thick towel or piece of folded blanket (to avoid the risk of fracture that comes with standing them on a cold surface). Tighten screw bands, wipe jars clean and leave to cool for about 8–12 hours.

Check seals by removing screw bands and lifting up each jar by the lid, or looking for depressions as explained previously under 'How Bottling Works' and 'Equipment', p 10.

Method 2 Quick water bath: jars filled with hot water or hot syrup

This is a speedier, simpler and less demanding way of bottling than Method 1 and I would recommend it to those who are new to preserving and somewhat worried by the complexities of temperatures, thermometers and so on.

Choose the same deep receptacle as given in Method 1. Pack fruit into jars. Fill with hot water or syrup. Fit on rubber rings, lids, clips and/or screw bands. If using screw bands, tighten fully then loosen by quarter-turn to allow air and steam to escape. (See 'How Bottling Works' and 'Equipment', p 10). Put into pan. Add sufficient warm water to cover jars completely. Bring water to simmering point over a period of 30 minutes. Simmer for length of time specified under individual entries.

Finish as directed in Method 1.

Method 3 Slow oven: jars filled, after heating, with boiling water or syrup

If you do not have a suitable receptacle, this is an easier method to negotiate than 1 or 2, although it is unsuitable for some fruits because the oven temperature is so low. These include light varieties such as peaches, pears and apples because they all discolour, in addition to 'solid pack' tomatoes and strawberries which have been left to soak overnight in syrup (see previous notes).

To prepare, line a baking tray with several thicknesses of newspaper or brown paper to catch spills. Set oven to 120°C (250°F), Gas ½, and pre-heat for ¼ hour. Pack jars with fruit as described earlier. Stand the jars on trays, making sure there is room around each so that they cannot knock together. Cover with glass lids or small saucers to prevent the top layer of fruit from scorching and/or over-cooking. *Do not* add rings, screw bands or clips as in other methods. Have an extra batch of fruit prepared in a jar for topping up others in case of shrinkage.

Process for length of time specified under individual entries, but make a note at this stage that the time is dependent on the type and amount of fruit being processed.

When cooking is complete, remove each jar from the oven. Stand jars on a wooden board or surface lined with several layers of newspaper or a thickish piece of folded blanket. Top up jars if necessary from the spare batch of fruit. Fill at once with boiling water or syrup then add rings, lids, clips or screw bands. Make sure screw bands are fully tightened. Wipe jars clean. Leave until completely cold before checking seals as described under 'How Bottling Works' and 'Equipment', p 10.

Method 4 Moderate oven: jars filled with boiling water or syrup before heating

Set oven to 150°C (300°F), Gas 2. Pre-heat ¼ hour. Prepare tray as in Method 3. Pack warm jars with fruit (remembering the extra one for topping up the others in case of shrinkage), and stand 5cm (2in) apart on trays. Fill with boiling water or syrup to within 2½cm (1in) of top. Add rubber rings

and lids etc, but *do not* put on screw bands.

Process for length of time specified under individual entries, making a note at this stage that the time depends on the type and amount of fruit being processed.

When cooking is complete, remove each jar carefully from the oven and stand on a wooden board or surface lined with either several layers of newspaper or a thick piece of folded blanket. Top up with fruit, etc, if necessary. Attach and tighten screw bands, wipe jars clean and leave until completely cold before checking seals as directed under 'How Bottling Works' and 'Equipment', p 10.

Method 5 Pressure cooking: jars filled with boiling water or syrup

This is a quick and economical way of bottling fruit, but it is essential that the cooker is fitted with a low weight not exceeding 2¼kg (5lb). Put the inverted rack into the cooker. Add jars packed with fruit (one or two depending on sizes and height), then fill with boiling water or syrup. Fit on rubber bands, lids etc, as directed in Methods 1 and 2, remembering to loosen screw bands by a quarter turn if used. Pour 2½cm (1in) *boiling* water into the cooker. Fit on lid but leave vent open.

Heat until steam can be seen coming out of vent. Add the weight, then bring up to pressure over a period of between 5 and 10 minutes. Maintain pressure for length of time specified under individual entries (for example, 1 minute for rhubarb; 4 minutes for plums; ¼ hour for tomatoes, etc).

Leave to cool down at kitchen temperature for 10 minutes, then stand cooker in sink. Run cold water over it to release remaining steam. Open lid. Remove jars, then continue as directed under Method 1.

Bottling Fruit Pulp

This is useful to store and can very easily be made and processed.

Cut up fruit and cook to a thick pulp or purée in just enough water to cover. Stir frequently to prevent burning. Add sugar at the very end or, if preferred, artificial sweetener. Reheat until bubbling.

Pack into warm jars and seal as fast as possible with rubber rings (taken straight out of boiling water), lids and screw bands which should be tightened up at once. Place bottles in water bath of hot water as described in Method 2, making sure they are completely immersed. Bring to the boil and boil for 5–6 minutes.

Remove carefully; wipe dry and cool. Store as directed for fruit.

Storing Bottled Fruit

Store jars in a cool, dry cupboard with no sign of dampness. Darkness is also essential, as a light environment bleaches or lightens the fruit. Check the seals periodically to ensure that they are still firmly fixed to the jars.

Using Bottled Fruit

Treat exactly as canned or stewed fruit. If re-heating, do so gently to prevent the fruit from breaking up.

Fruit Bottling with Chemicals

It is not always possible to bottle fruit by heat sterilisation and the next best thing for some fruits is sulphur dioxide, available from specialist pharmacies and DIY wine-making departments of stores etc, under the name of Camden Fruit Preserving tablets.

Choice of Fruits

The best are hard and semi-hard fruits, and include plums, damsons, greengages and apples. Soft fruits are best processed by other methods and fruits to avoid altogether are dessert cherries, tomatoes and pears. No vegetables at all should be preserved with Camden tablets.

Method

Prepare sound and slightly under-ripe fruit according to type. Pack into glass or stone jars. Fill with sulphur dioxide solution, made by stirring Camden tablets in warm or cold water until dissolved. The usual proportion is 1 tablet to 275ml ($\frac{1}{2}$pt) water and this amount should be sufficient for $\frac{1}{2}$kg (1lb) fruit. It is important to ensure that the fruit is completely covered with the Camden solution. If not, make up more and add.

Covering

It is essential to close jars so that each one is airtight. Therefore cover with Porosan Skin tied down tightly, or with a piece of cloth dipped in melted mutton fat or paraffin wax. This, too, should be tied to the jar securely *before* it has hardened. Afterwards more melted fat or wax should be painted over the cloth.

Storage

Store in a cool, dark and dry cupboard.

Using

As soon as you open the jar, you will notice that the liquid smells strongly of sulphur and the fruit itself has lost colour. To remedy, tip contents into a saucepan and, in an airy room, boil the fruit and liquid together for 10 minutes, *keeping the pan uncovered* throughout. The smell of sulphur should disappear in this time and the colour of the fruit should return. Add sugar to taste (or artificial sweetener), and continue to stew gently until the fruit is cooked.

Serve as it is with cream or custard, or use in pies, puddings, crumbles etc. *Never* eat the fruit until it has first been cooked as just described.

'Granny receipts' for bottling are often not to be recommended now that we have more certain methods. But they have their interest . . .

Wax for Bottles

2 parts of beeswax, 1 part of resin, 1 part powdered colour (Venetian red). Melt the beeswax and resin in an old iron saucepan. (Only melt, do not boil.) Then stir in the colour and let it cool a little, both to avoid the pungent vapours and to thicken slightly. Dip the corked tops of the bottles while holding them horizontally over the pot, and turn them round, so as to run the extra stuff into the joint; they are the better for a second dip. Leave the remains of the wax to harden in the pot, which should be used for this purpose only. It can be melted again at any time, and more added as wanted.

Bottled Green Gooseberries

Pick off noses and stalks, but be careful not to burst the berries. Then fill some wide-mouthed bottles quite full, tie over the mouths paper with pricked holes, stand the bottles in boiling water, and just let the fruit turn colour (no sugar or anything with the fruit). Take the bottles out, and cork and seal them. The old way was to bury them head downwards in a garden border; but if well sealed, to keep out all air, I do not believe that is necessary. Green Currants are excellent done the same way, and Morella Cherries, small Plums, and Damsons; only these must be ripe.

From Mrs C. W. Earle's *Pot-Pourri From a Surrey Garden* (c 1899)

To Preserve Fruit for Tarts, or Family Desserts

Cherries, plums of all sorts, and American apples, gather when ripe, and lay them in small jars that will hold a pound; strew over each jar six ounces of good loaf sugar, pounded; cover with two bladders each, separately tied down; then set the jars in a large stewpan of water up to the neck, and let it boil three hours gently. Keep these and all others sorts of fruit free from damp.

To Bottle Black Currants

Top and tail the currants, and when the bottles are filled, add one tablespoonful of gin. Keep in a cool and dry place, and either resin the corks, or tie them over with bladders.

From J. H. Walsh, *Domestic Economy* (c 1877)

2
Candied Peel

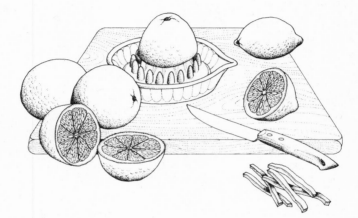

The peel of any fruits of the citrus family can be candied fairly easily at home, and will make an unusual after-dinner sweetmeat with coffee.

Wash fruit thoroughly and scrub if necessary to remove any dirty marks from its pores. Halve fruit and squeeze out juice. (The juice can be kept for breakfast drinks, etc.) Remove pulp from squeezed halves by scraping it out with a spoon or curved grapefruit knife. Discard. Cut peel into narrowish strips. Put into saucepan. Cover well with water. Bring to boil. Lower heat. Cover. Simmer between 1 and 2 hours or until peel is tender.

If cooking grapefruit peel, change water two or three times to reduce bitterness.

Drain thoroughly and reserve 275ml (½pt) liquor, adding extra water if necessary. Pour into pan. Add 225g (8oz) caster sugar. Melt over a low heat, stirring. Bring to boil, stir in peel, then take off heat. Leave peel to stand in the syrup for two days.

Drain off syrup and pour into clean pan. Add 125g (4oz) caster sugar. Dissolve slowly, add peel and simmer gently in syrup until it becomes semi-transparent and most of the syrup has been absorbed. Cover pan when cold and leave peel to stand in the syrup for 2 to 3 weeks.

To dry, take peel out of pan and spread on to a baking sheet lined with non-stick parchment paper. Place in a cool oven set to 50°C (120°F), Gas ½. Leave to dry until surfaces of peel are no longer sticky to the touch. Turn pieces over from time to time. The whole process may take from 2 to 4 hours.

Toss in granulated sugar and, when cold, store in airtight containers.

Note: If candied peel is being made in the summer, and you happen to hit a dry, clear and hot day, put the peel outside and leave the sun to do the drying.

3
Chutney

Chutney – and mango chutney in particular – dates back to the latter part of the nineteenth and first half of this century and was introduced to Britain by 'colonials' who first enjoyed these sweet-sour condiments while resident in India during the time of the raj. The popularity of chutney – or sweet pickle – has never waned as an accompaniment to curries, cold meats, poultry, cheese, pies and sausages, and even the method of making has changed little since 1888 when Isabella Beeton described chutney as 'a powerful condiment, prepared by mixing a variety of fruits, sugar and spices in such an able manner that no particular flavour predominates.'

There is little I can add to describe chutney better, other than to say that chutneys are only as powerful as the amount of cayenne pepper you choose to add, and that in general a good chutney is one in which all the ingredients meld together in an atmosphere of harmony and understanding.

Equipment

To prevent a metallic tang permeating the chutney, it should be cooked in enamel, stainless steel or aluminium. Pans made of copper, brass and iron should be avoided. For the same reasons, I find the best and safest implement with which to stir the chutney is a wooden spoon, or a spatula made of rigid plastic.

Ingredients

Fruit
The choice is infinite and literally any fruit – even bananas – can form the basis of a successful and appetising chutney. Generally, the most popular are apples, green and red tomatoes, gooseberries and plums.

Vegetables
The most usual vegetable is onions.

Flavourings
Salt and garlic add the necessary savoury touches to chutneys, together with cinnamon, ground ginger, mixed spices, cloves, mace, bay leaves and cayenne pepper to taste.

Sweetness
This comes from the addition of dried fruit – chopped dates, sultanas and/or raisins, with stem or crystallised ginger – varying amounts of sugar and sometimes a little black treacle.

Colour
A dark chutney is often one to which soft brown sugar has been added with, sometimes, a small amount of black treacle. A lighter chutney is one where white sugar instead of dark has been used.

Sharpness
This is contributed by vinegar and the one most frequently used is good quality malt.

Preparing Ingredients

For smoothness, evenness and uniformity of flavour, the fresh fruit and vegetables should be finely chopped or coarsely minced. The small dried fruits, which give chutneys their special character, should be added whole, but dates and stem ginger should be cut into pieces the size of sultanas.

Where spices are recommended, these refer to ground-up or powdered varieties. If whole spices are used – ginger and cinnamon sticks for example – 'bruise' them by tapping lightly with a hammer to extract as much flavour as possible. They should then, with the pickling spices, be tied in a piece of clean cloth and added to the chutney.

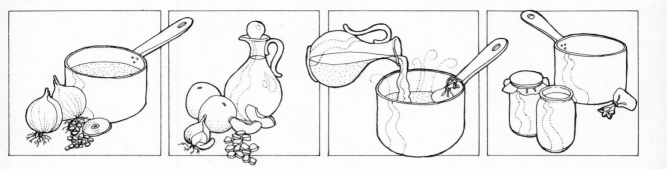

Cooking

As vinegar is known to have a toughening effect on vegetables in general and on onions in particular, it is advisable to simmer the onions, with just enough water to cover, in a large saucepan with a close-fitting lid for about $\frac{1}{4}$ hour *before* adding the other ingredients.

The length of time it takes to cook the chutney depends very much on the type of fruit etc used, the strength of heat under the saucepan and the size of the pan itself; the contents in a broad-based, shallow pan will cook down far more quickly than they would in a tall and narrow one.

For a mature-flavoured, deep toned and thickish chutney, the ingredients should be slowly brought to the boil and then allowed to simmer, uncovered, for about $2-2\frac{1}{2}$ hours. It is important to stir periodically with a large wooden spoon, as chutney can stick to the base of the pan fairly easily and give a burnt flavour to the whole batch.

Bottling and Storage

Bottle, cover and store as directed for jam but keep the chutney 4–6 months before eating so that the flavour has time to develop and mature. Porosan Skin tied over the neck of each jar makes an excellent cover, but please be guided by directions which come with each pack.

As metal is corroded by the vinegar in chutney, avoid covering the jars with metal lids unless they are well-lacquered and/or lined with vinegar-resistant paper.

'Hot' Chutney

The fire in a chutney, as I said earlier, is dependent on how much cayenne pepper is added to it. For mild chutneys, add none at all. For chutneys with a bit of a kick, add about $\frac{1}{2}$ level teaspoon to each batch. For hot chutneys, adjust the amount of cayenne pepper according to personal taste.

Chutney recipes from Victorian cooks:

A Cucumber and Onion Chutney

The following fresh chutney is good with any roast or cold meat:—
Equal parts of cucumber, onion, and sultanas chopped very fine, some
salt and cayenne. Moisten with vinegar, and press for two hours. It
will keep some time: when wanted for use, warm in a little gravy and
let it get cold.

From Mrs. C. W. Earle's *Pot-Pourri From a Surrey Garden* (c 1899)

Tomato Chutney

Five pounds of tomatoes, one pound of moist sugar, half an ounce of
garlic, one quart of vinegar. Boil in an enamelled pan to a pulp and
rub through a tammy. Add one pound of chopped sultanas, two
ounces of mustard seeds, three ounces of salt, one ounce of ground
ginger, a quarter of an ounce of cayenne. Mix well and bottle. Wax the
corks.

Apple Chutney

Four pounds of apples, two pounds of moist sugar, one ounce of
garlic, two quarts of brown vinegar. Wash and wipe the apples but do
not pare them; cut them up and boil the above ingredients until soft,
then rub through a hair sieve. Add one pound and a half of chopped
raisins, four ounces of salt, two ounces of mustard seeds, two ounces of
ground ginger, a quarter of an ounce of cayenne. Mix well and bottle;
cork securely.

From Mary Pope, *Novel Dishes for Vegetarian Households* (c 1893)

4
Drying

Drying, and salting, are two of the earliest methods of preservation and, even today, areas of the world still dry their fish, meat, fruit, vegetables and herbs by natural means: sun-drying which, with certain air streams, gives many foods their characteristic flavour, colour and texture. Just think of genuine Parma ham.

Drying is possibly best carried out in a country with a hot and dry climate rather than a temperate and damp one; all the same, many people do like to dry their own fruits, vegetables and herbs come what may. For those of you who are keen to try this particular art of preservation which, I have to admit, is relatively uncomplicated, here are the facts.

For home drying, there are three essentials: correct temperature (normally the oven unless otherwise specified), adequate ventilation or circulation of air, and special trays on which to dry the fruit, etc.

The trays themselves are neither costly nor complicated and can be made at home by any DIY enthusiast. All that needs doing is to nail together, in a square, four wooden laths and then stretch fine wire mesh or cheesecloth across the framework. The wire mesh base is the more practical proposition, because once it is made it lasts almost a lifetime, and all you then have to do is cover it before use with a piece of well-washed and dried cheesecloth. It is important to note that new cheesecloth contains dressing which scorches easily, and it must therefore be washed thoroughly before use.

The Oven and Heat
The fruit or leaves, etc, can be dried consistently in the oven at a controlled temperature, or dried intermittently in residual heat coming from a solid-fuel oven. Both methods give satisfactory results.

Fruit
The fruit should be in perfect condition and very fresh. Ripe fruit dries more quickly than under-ripe, keeps a better colour and has a vastly improved flavour. The fruit should be prepared according to type (see individual entries), arranged on the trays and dried at a temperature of between 50°C/66°C (120/150°F), Gas ½/2, for the times specified under the entry for each individual fruit. (General directions for drying herbs follow, p 25.)

It is best to keep to the lower temperature for a few hours at the beginning to stop the outside of the fruit from hardening: once hardening has taken place, it makes the process of drying slower by preventing evaporation of moisture from the centre of the fruit. Where plums for example are concerned, if the initial heat is low the skins are less likely to split.

After the fruit has been removed from the oven, it should be left to cool at ordinary kitchen temperature for about 12 hours. Subsequently it should be packed into cardboard or wooden boxes lined with greaseproof paper, lightly covered with more paper and stored in a very dry place; provided space permits, a linen cupboard is ideal.

On no account should the dried fruit be in an airtight container as it will sweat and deteriorate.

Using
Before cooking, all dried fruits should be well washed, put into a bowl and covered with water. The bowl should be protected from dust by covering it with a saucepan lid or plate. The fruit should be left to soak for 24 hours and then simmered gently until tender in the water in which it was soaked. Sugar to taste should be added at the very end, after the fruit has softened.

Vegetables

While most vegetables can be dried, roots such as carrots, swedes, etc, are best left stored in sand or clamps and should not undergo the drying process suggested below for other vegetables. In addition, I would avoid drying peas because the results rarely justify the effort involved. Probably the two most satisfactory vegetables to tackle – especially for novices – are beans and mushrooms and directions for both follow.

Beans

The best for the purpose of drying are young and fresh dwarf or runner beans. Dwarf beans can be topped and tailed, have their side strings removed and then dried whole. Runner beans should be prepared in the same way and then cut diagonally into thin strips with a stainless knife or a bean-slicing machine. They should then be tied in a large piece of washed cheesecloth or placed in a wire basket, lowered into a large pan of boiling water and blanched for between 2 and 5 minutes, depending on their age. The beans should be removed from the water, and spread out on trays. They should then be put into a cool oven set to 50°C (120°F), Gas ½, and the temperature increased a few degrees over ½ hour until it reaches 66°C (150°F), Gas 2. Cooking should be continued until the beans are crisp. They should then be left to cool completely in the dryest place available. Transfer them to stoppered jars or bottles and store in a dark, dry place.

Before cooking dried beans, soak them in plenty of cold water for 12 hours, then cook in boiling salted water until tender.

Mushrooms

Choose the freshest possible mushrooms (or any other edible fungi) and peel if necessary. Also remove stalks. Spread out on trays. Alternatively, thread on to lengths of string before placing on trays. Dry out for several hours in a low oven set to 50°C (120°F), Gas ½, until very dry and crisp. Store as beans.

Herbs

The most satisfactory herbs for drying are those most commonly used: parsley, mint, sage, marjoram, winter savory and thyme. The technique is as follows:

1 Pick herbs while still young and just about to flower. They should be absolutely dry and *not* have been exposed to sunlight.
2 Herbs with small leaves, such as thyme and savory, should be bundled together, well washed, shaken dry and protected with a covering of cheesecloth. The bundles should be hung up to dry, leaves pointing downwards, in a very dry place.
3 If you are dealing with large-leafed herbs – sage for example – strip leaves off stalks, tie in a piece of cheesecloth and plunge for 1 minute in a large pan of boiling water.
4 Remove from pan, shake away surplus water and spread leaves out on trays.
5 Dry out for between 1 and 1½ hours in a cool oven set to 50°C (120°F), Gas ½. When drying is completed, the leaves should be crisp and crumbly.
6 Crush with a rolling pin and store in well-stoppered jars away from light; preferably in a dark cupboard.

There is nothing new in drying herbs. But when it comes to preserving fruit in moss – most of us will not try this one!

To prepare sweet Herbs for keeping

It is highly desirable, according to the taste and style of living of the family, that preparations of sweet herbs, either in powder, dried bunches (the powder is best), or in the form of essences and tinctures, be always kept at hand, ready for use. The following is the best way of preparing them:—Gather your herbs, including thyme of the various sorts, marjoram and savoury, sage, mint, and balm, hyssop and pennyroyal, when they are come to full growth, just before they begin to flower; when they must be gathered perfectly free from damp, dust, dirt, and insects. Cut off the roots, and tie the herbs in small bundles. Dry as quick as possible, either in the sun, in a dutch oven before the fire, or in a dry room with a thorough draught. When quite dry, pick off the leaves, and rub them till they are reduced to a fine powder, when bottle close for use. Seeds of parsley, fennel, and celery, should be kept for the purpose of flavouring, when the green herb cannot be obtained.

From W. G. Lewis, *The Cook* (19th century)

To store Fruit

Those to be used first, lay by singly on shelves, or on the floor, in a dry southern room, on clean dry moss, or sweet dry straw, so as not to touch one another. Some, or all the rest, having first laid a fortnight singly, and then nicely culled, are to be spread on shelves, or on a dry floor. But the most superior way is, to pack in large earthen, or China or stone jars, with very dry long moss at the bottom, sides, and also between them, if it might be. Press a good coat of moss on the top, and then stop the mouth close with a cork, or otherwise, which should be rosined round about with a twentieth part of bees' wax in it. As the object is effectually to keep out air (the cause of putrefaction), the jars, if earthen, may be set on dry sand, which put also between, round, and over them, to a foot thick on the top. In all close storing, observe there should be no doubt of the soundness of the fruit. Guard, in time, from frost those that lie open. Jars of fruit must be soon used after unsealing.

From *The Practical Housewife* by the Editor of *The Family Friend* (c 1880)

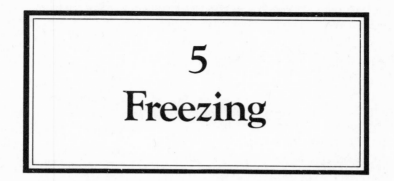

5
Freezing

Freezing goes back to the very earliest times when people living in Arctic climates buried food in holes dug out of ice – improvised deep-freezes of a kind – and left it there for months on end, knowing it would be as good as new when hacked out and cooked. Thus what we think of as a comparatively new method of preservation is as old as the proverbial hills and is one of the safest, most hygienic and most effective methods of storing fresh food for long periods with minimal, if any, deterioration.

Domestic deep-freezes operate at a temperature of —18°C (0°F), which is cold enough to prevent or slow down the development and growth of bacteria damaging to food. As a result, fruit and vegetables, as well as meat, fish, dairy produce and made-up dishes, stay naturally fresh and there is little spoilage of flavour, texture, appearance and nutritional value.

Freezing is especially recommended for fruit, vegetables and herbs and, provided all varieties are pre-treated as described below, there is very little to go wrong. What *is* important is sound packaging and secure sealing. With such an enormous choice of freezer accessories and freezer information available from freezer centres, stationers, supermarkets and department stores, this should present few problems – even to the novice.

Freezer – Not Fridge

What I must emphasise, however, is this. A freezing compartment in a refrigerator is *not* the same as a domestic deep-freeze (marked, as a general rule, with one large and three smaller stars) and should never be used for deep-freezing foods you have prepared yourself from scratch. The reason is clear. The temperature in the compartment is *above* —18°C (0°F) and is therefore too high to do a satisfactory job of fast freezing. Refrigerator freezing compartments are designed only to store *already* deep-frozen foods and the length of time they may be kept depends on the star markings on the cabinet. With one star, you can store foods for one week; two stars, one month; three stars, three months. If, for convenience, your domestic deep-freeze is in a garage, or in another area in the house, frozen foods from it (such as home-cooked anything as well as packets of commercially frozen foods) can be transferred to the freezing compartment of the refrigerator, which is probably housed in the kitchen.

Freezing Vegetables

Enzymes are present in all vegetables and, in order to prevent spoilage of flavour, texture, appearance and nutritional value, their action has to be stopped. Hence blanching, which is carried out as follows:

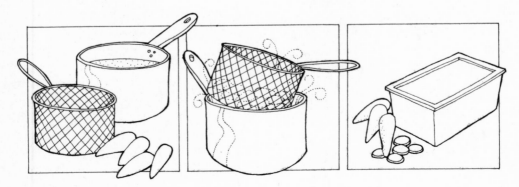

Blanching

1 Select a large saucepan of about 4½ litres (8pt) capacity (larger if liked but certainly no smaller). Two-thirds fill with water and bring to a galloping boil.

2 Place ½kg (1lb) prepared vegetables into a wire basket, metal sieve or colander. Lower carefully into boiling water. Blanch for length of time given for each vegetable under individual entries. (Times vary from about 2 to 10 minutes.)

3 Start timing the process *after* the water in the pan has returned to a rapid boil. Lift basket etc of vegetables out of the pan. Shake to remove surplus hot water. Rinse under cold running water or alternatively tip into large bowl of iced water.

4 Drain vegetables thoroughly. Pack and store as directed under individual entries.

Note: In the absence of a large pan, blanch half the amount of vegetables in a pan containing 2¼ litres (4pt) of water.

'Free Flow' Freezing of Vegetables

When vegetables are frozen by the 'free flow' method ('open freezing'), each one – be it a pea or a baby carrot – is individually frozen and will subsequently remain separate during storage. This is a very practical method in that specific amounts may be taken out of the pack or container as necessary (an individual portion for example), while the remainder can be returned to the freezer for future use.

1 Spread out previously blanched vegetables on wire racks or a flat baking sheet and *leave uncovered*.

2 Fast freeze for 1 to 2 hours or until vegetables are hard and just beginning to look frosted.

3 Pack quickly into bags or containers. Return to and store in the freezer.

Packing speedily is essential, otherwise the vegetables will begin to thaw and stick together in clumps.

Cooking Frozen Vegetables

All vegetables can be cooked from frozen (in fact I think the flavour and texture are better than if they are thawed), but the time of cooking should be reduced by the time originally allowed for blanching. Therefore if the vegetables require 7 minutes to cook and were blanched for 2 minutes, the cooking time becomes only 5 minutes.

Storage Times

Most firm vegetables can be frozen for up to one year. Watery ones – like marrow and mushrooms – should be used up sooner, so please be guided by individual entries.

Storing Unblanched Vegetables

Although blanching is always recommended, vegetables may be frozen unblanched, but then they must be used up within 2 months. This is because they lose flavour and Vitamin C if stored for a longer period of time. Carrots are the exception to this rule: they can be left unblanched and then stored satisfactorily in the freezer for up to 9 months.

Vegetable Purées

To purée cooked vegetables, blend to a smooth purée in blender goblet, adding a small amount of stock, water or milk if necessary – which means if the vegetables in the blender start clogging up because they are too dry. Add seasonings to taste while the vegetables are blending. Pack and store in rigid containers, leaving 2½cm (1in) headroom for expansion; or alternatively pack in polythene bags, tying loosely at the top to allow for expansion.

Vegetables Unsuitable for Freezing

Green, leafy salad vegetables become limp and not particularly palatable, so do not freeze lettuce, cress or cucumber.

Freezing Herbs

At one time the only way of storing herbs was to dry them. Now freezing makes good, practical sense and the two most usual methods are given here.

Method 1
1 Wash fresh herbs thoroughly. Chop finely.
2 Pack ice-cube trays fitted with dividers two-thirds full with herbs. Top up with water.
3 Fast freeze until hard. Remove frozen herb cubes from trays.
4 Transfer to polythene bags, keeping each variety separate.
5 Secure bag or bags and store up to one year.

To use, either thaw cube or cubes in fine mesh sieve and allow to drain completely; or alternatively add whole cubes to stews, casseroles and sauces, etc. If a cube is being added to a white sauce, reduce the amount of liquid added to the roux of fat and flour by about 1 to 1½ tablespoons.

Method 2
1 Wash and dry fresh herbs.
2 Remove leaves from stalks if large (sage and mint for example). Leave in sprays if leaves are small (thyme and basil).
3 Place small amounts into squares of cling film or foil. Wrap, seal and label. Alternatively, put into small-size polythene bags. Seal well and label.
4 Freeze until hard. Store up to one year.

To use, crumble herbs into little bits while still frozen, and then chopping will be completely unnecessary. Use as fresh herbs, but be careful with thyme and sage as they develop a very full flavour when frozen, and should therefore be added sparingly and with care.

Freezing Fruit

The major advantage of freezing fresh fruits is that one is able to enjoy out-of-season varieties all through the year, and also make the best possible use of home-grown produce and sudden gluts which appear unexpectedly both in one's own garden and in local shops or market stalls.

As for jam and bottling, fruit for freezing must be in prime condition and under-ripe; badly marked fruit should be avoided, as the colour and flavour will be unsatisfactory. There are three main methods of freezing fruit:

Method 1: 'Free Flow'
This equates to the 'free flow' freezing of vegetables and exactly the same principles apply. Therefore see page 29 and read fruit for vegetables. Summer fruits – especially whole strawberries, raspberries and strings of currants – are often treated this way if they are wanted for decoration, although it must be remembered that once thawed, the fruits do tend to sag.

Method 2: Freezing in Syrup

This is recommended for fruits which discolour fairly quickly once they are peeled and sliced and left in the atmosphere. Into this group fall apples, pears, peaches and apricots. I also favour syrup for sour plums and damsons because it seems to improve their colour and flavour.

There are three strengths of syrup used for fruit and you can choose which you prefer: it depends on the sharpness of the fruit itself and your personal taste in sweetness.

Syrup 1 (30%; light): Use 225g (8oz) caster sugar to 575ml (1pt) water.

Syrup 2 (40%; medium): Use 375g (13oz) caster sugar to 575ml (1pt) water.

Syrup 3 (50%; heavy): Use 575g (1¼lb) caster sugar to 575ml (1pt) water.

To make, pour the water into the pan. Add the sugar. Stir over low heat until sugar dissolves. Boil for one minute only. Remove from heat. Leave until completely cold.

To prevent fruit from discolouring at all during storage, add ¼ level teaspoon ascorbic acid (available from pharmacies) to every 575ml (1pt) *cold* syrup.

To pack, half-fill rigid containers with syrup. Add prepared fruit, leaving about 2½cm (1in) headroom for expansion. Cover, seal and label.

Store up to 1 year for stoned fruit; 6 months for fruit with stones. As a general guide, 275ml (½pt) syrup should be adequate to cover ½kg (1lb) of fruit.

Note: To prevent fruit from rising up in the containers, place some crumpled polythene or greaseproof paper directly over the fruit and syrup before covering with the lid etc. To thaw, leave uncovered containers for 6 to 8 hours in the refrigerator, or 2 to 4 hours at room temperature.

Method 3: Layering with Sugar

This is the best method for dealing with soft fruits such as strawberries, raspberries, loganberries, currants etc.

Gently toss ½kg (1lb) prepared fruit with 125g (4oz) caster sugar. Pack into rigid containers, leaving 1¼cm (½in) headroom for expansion. Cover, seal and label.

To thaw, leave uncovered containers 4 to 6 hours in the refrigerator or 2 to 3 hours at

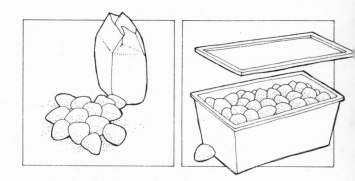

room temperature. The fruit is best eaten just before it has completely thawed.

Note: Granulated sugar may be used in preference to caster, but the fruit will take longer to thaw and may taste a little more crunchy.

Fruit Purées

These freeze beautifully, hold for 12 months and are extremely useful all the year round for making mousses, soufflés, ice creams, fools, sauces and innumerable hot and cold desserts.

Note: It is useful to know that sugar need not be added to fruit purées; diabetics and those on low-sugar diets can use artificial sweetener or none at all.

Method 1
Blend soft fruit or fruits to a purée in your mixer goblet, adding lemon juice to those varieties which are liable to discolour. Sweeten to taste with sifted icing sugar, or leave unsweetened. In the absence of a blender, mash fruit finely or rub through a fine nylon sieve, adding lemon juice if necessary. Again sweeten to taste with sifted icing sugar if desired.

Spread smoothly into rigid containers, leaving 2½cm (1in) headroom for expansion. Alternatively, store in polythene bags, tying loosely at the top so that there is enough room for expansion.

Method 2
Cook prepared fruit until very soft in just enough water to prevent burning. Blend to a smooth purée in blender goblet, adding sugar to taste or leaving unsweetened. Pack as directed in Method 1.

Fruits Unsuitable for Freezing

Avocado pears and bananas.

Preserving in Ice
Ice is the most useful of all the means of preserving meats and fish in a fresh state, with or without the aid of salt. Here we have to consider ice as a means of keeping fish, creams, &c., in a fresh state.

Refrigerator
In order to keep this ice for some days, the ice company sell a refrigerator or portable ice-chest, which is a very efficient instrument, though not, perhaps, quite coming up to the description given by its proprietors.

For icing wines, the refrigerators possess peculiar advantages; the temperature to be imparted to wine can be regulated at pleasure, and if more wine be iced at any time than is required for the particular occasion, it is neither wasted nor injured, as it can be left for any period in the refrigerator without deterioration. To ice wine it is necessary merely to place it in the refrigerator; and the temperature can be regulated by the length of time during which it is suffered to remain.

From J. H. Walsh, *Domestic Economy* (c 1877)

6
Fruits in Alcohol

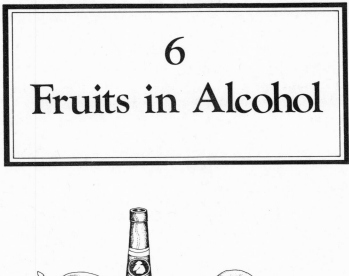

Fruits preserved in alcohol look and taste luxurious and are much less costly to make at home than they are to buy in high-quality food shops. This section includes a short selection of recipes which you may be inspired to try when certain spirits are on 'special offer' or you have just returned from a trip abroad with your duty-free allowance.

Rum Pot

My favourite – and indeed everybody's favourite once they have tasted it – is Germany's Rumtopf or Rum Pot which begins life in May and ends around October, using on its way all fruits in season from spring to autumn. Below is a translation worked out and adapted slightly by me.

'It takes a long time to complete a Rum Pot, but the actual making of it is child's play. You need, first of all, a *large* stone jar or earthenware crock, fruit, sugar and dark rum. The fruit should be ripe – but not over-ripe – unblemished and well washed and dried.

1 Combine ½kg (1lb) fruit with 250g (9oz) caster sugar and place in the jar. Leave for one hour, then gently pour over 1 litre (1¾pt) of dark rum. Every time another batch of fruit and sugar is added (proportion as above every time), it will probably be necessary to top up with some extra rum to keep the fruits immersed in alcohol all the time. Do not dilute the rum or the Rum Pot will be spoiled and may then deteriorate.

2 To prevent fruit from rising in the jar, place a clean and non-metallic plate over the top. Cover with waxed paper or polythene and leave in a cool dark place. Check level of rum in the pot frequently. There should be a finger thickness covering the fruit. If not, add some extra rum – never water!

3 Which fruits to choose? From late May to June, start with ½kg (1lb) strawberries, 250g (9oz) sugar and 1 litre (1¾pt) of rum. From June to July, cherries and, if possible, unstoned Morello or 'sour' cherries which have a very distinctive flavour; otherwise use any dessert cherries available. From July to August, halved or quartered unpeeled peaches and apricots. From August to September, halved and stoned ripe plums and greengages (not damsons). From September to October, large cubes of peeled, cored and diced dessert pears, and pieces of fresh pineapple.

4 Four weeks after the last fruits have been added to the pot, pour in another ½ litre (⅞pt) of rum. Leave to stand, covered, for a further 2 weeks.'

I usually stir the contents round with a wooden stick before eating so that all the fruits are mixed together instead of settling in layers.

This is a superb confection and if the amount of rum sounds harrowing and ridiculously extravagant, may I point out that a little Rum Pot goes a very long way and, spooned into small jars and prettily covered, it makes ideal gifts for Christmas and the New Year.

Using Rum Pot
It can be eaten alone as a treat on cold winter days; served as an accompaniment to Russian tea; spooned over ice cream and topped with whipped cream; used as a very special sauce with steamed or baked sponge puddings; packed inside pancakes.

Note: Raspberries, gooseberries, loganberries and blackcurrants may be added to taste, but they can become somewhat mushy on standing.

Prunes in Armagnac

This is a French speciality and you can keep the whole thing going for ages by topping up the jar with extra prunes and Armagnac every time you take some out!

Fill one or two attractive glass jars with large prunes. Slowly add Armagnac until it reaches the brims. Cover securely, and again I would recommend Porosan Skin. Leave to stand for about two months before eating. Once opened, protect contents by covering jar/jars with cling film. Dried dates (stoned) may be used instead of prunes.

Figs in Whisky

Follow exactly the same method as Prunes in Armagnac, but substitute dried figs for prunes. A level teaspoon of finely grated orange peel added to the contents of each jar does magical things to the flavour.

Peaches in Brandy

Make a heavy syrup by dissolving, over a low heat, 1kg (2lb) caster sugar in $\frac{3}{4}$ litre (1$\frac{1}{4}$pt) water. Add 2 teaspoons lemon juice, bring to the boil and boil gently for $\frac{1}{4}$ hour.

Remove skins of about 12 medium peaches by plunging the fruit into hot water, leaving for 2 minutes and draining, then rinsing under cold water.

When skins are removed, cut each peach in half, then take out and discard stones. Poach peach halves, a few at a time, in the syrup. Allow about 5 minutes cooking time but watch carefully in case the fruit starts breaking up. Baste frequently unless peach halves are completely immersed.

Lift out of syrup with a draining spoon and transfer to suitable glass jars which should be warmed first.

Boil remaining syrup until fairly thick but *do not* allow it to turn brown or even golden, otherwise you will end up with toffee! Pour the syrup into a measuring cup, leave until cold then mix with an equal amount of brandy. Use to fill up jars, adding extra brandy until liquid reaches brims. Cover securely when cold. (For covering instructions, see Prunes in Armagnac).

Leave for about one month in a cool, dark, dry place before eating in the same ways as Rum Pot.

Apricots in Brandy

Treat exactly the same as peaches.

Cherries in Brandy

Toss $\frac{1}{2}$kg (1lb) stalked Morello cherries in 575g (1$\frac{1}{4}$lb) caster sugar. Pack into clean, dry jars, adding any left-over sugar. Top up with brandy. Cover. (For covering instructions, see Prunes in Armagnac.)

Leave 3–4 months before eating.

Note: All these fruits may be preserved in Calvados (French apple brandy) instead of grape brandy.

Preserving Fruits in alcohol is an interesting adventure. Tincture of Seville orange peel may not be everyone's choice, but the brandy Grapes could interest anyone who has already tried the apricots and peaches.

Apricots or Peaches in brandy

Wipe and weigh the fruit, and prick them, and take a quarter of the weight of fine powdered sugar; put the fruit into an ice-pot that shuts very close, throw the sugar over it, and then cover the fruit with brandy. Between the top and cover of the pot, put a piece of double cap-paper. Set the pot into a saucepan of water till the brandy be as hot as you can possibly bear to put your finger in, but it must not boil. Put the fruit into a jar, and pour the brandy on it. When cold, put a bladder over, and tie it down tight.

Cherries in brandy

Weigh the finest Morellos, having cut off half the stalk; prick them with a new needle, and drop them into a jar or wide-mouthed bottle. Pound three-quarters the weight of sugar or white candy; strew, fill up with brandy, and tie a bladder over them.

Tincture of Lemon or Seville Orange Peel

Half fill a wide-mouthed bottle with good spirits; shave the thin rind off the lemon, and put it into the bottle until it is full: it may be either strained off into bottles, or suffered to remain on the rind.

From W. G. Lewis, *The Cook* (19th century)

To Preserve Strawberries in Wine

Put a quantity of the finest large strawberries into a gooseberry bottle, and strew in three large spoonfuls of fine sugar; fill up with Madeira wine, or fine sherry.

Brandy Grapes

For this purpose the grapes should be in large close bunches, and quite ripe. Remove every grape that is the least shrivelled, or in any way defective; with a needle prick each grape in three places; have ready a sufficiency of double-refined loaf sugar, powdered and sifted; put some of the sugar into the bottom of the jars, then put in a bunch of grapes and cover all thickly with sugar, then another bunch, then more sugar, and so on till the jar is nearly full, finishing with a layer of sugar; then fill up to the top with the best white brandy; cover the jars as closely as possible, and set them away; they must not go over the fire; the grapes should be of the best quality, either white or purple.

From J. H. Walsh, *Domestic Economy* (c 1877)

7
Fruit Cheeses, Butters and Curds

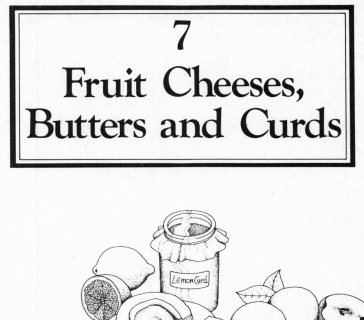

Fruit cheeses – and fruit butters – are lovely, country confections made and appreciated in rural areas and sometimes served in place of cheese for high tea, or as an accompaniment to duckling, goose and game. They are well worth making when supplies of fruit are plentiful, as happens every so often, and you do not want to waste any of the season's crop.

Choice of Fruits

Almost any fruit can be used, but those most recommended are apples, blackcurrants, damsons, medlars and quinces.

Fruit Cheeses

Preparation of Fruit

Wash and dry fruit, removing and discarding any spoiled and damaged portions. Coarsely chop fruit (with damsons it is not necessary to remove stones, simply slit each one) and put into pan.

Add sufficient water to come halfway up the fruit. Bring to the boil. Lower heat. Cover. Simmer about 1 hour or until fruit is very soft and pulpy. Rub through fine-mesh sieve. If resultant purée looks very thin, boil briskly to reduce down to a somewhat thickish consistency. Stir frequently to reduce sticking.

Cooking the Cheese

Allow ½kg (1lb) sugar to every ½kg (1lb) fruit purée. Put into heavy based pan. Stir over low heat until all the sugar has completely dissolved.

Continue to cook very slowly, stirring often in a figure of eight movement, until the contents are *very thick*. This can take anything from 1 to 2 hours. The cheese is ready when a spoon drawn across the centre leaves a clean and straight line.

Potting

Transfer the fruit cheese to small moulds brushed with glycerine or corn oil. Cover exactly as for jam. To serve, turn out on to a dish, cut into wedges and serve as suggested earlier, or use as an accompaniment to mild Cheddar cheese and bread and butter. Store as for jam.

Fruit Butters

These are softer in texture than the cheeses and although they can be used for exactly the same purposes, they do not hold as well and should therefore be stored in a refrigerator, dry cellar or really cold and well-ventilated larder or pantry. They are generally spiced – for example, apple with cinnamon.

Make exactly as the cheeses but reduce

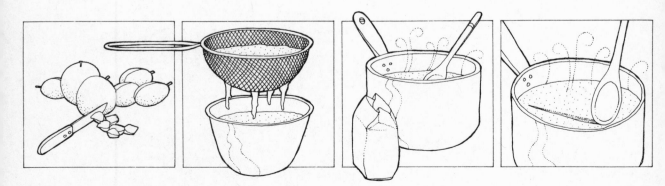

the quantity of sugar to fruit pulp by 125g (4oz). Therefore allow 350g (12oz) sugar to ½kg (1lb) pulp.

Ideally they should be covered with air-tight covers, but this can be a fairly complicated process. Instead I cover fruit butters as for jam and then store them in the refrigerator for up to 3 months. They are best eaten as a substitute for jam – with bread and butter or scones, in pancakes etc.

Fruit Curds

These are not by definition a fruit preserve, mixed as they are with butter and eggs. Nevertheless Lemon Curd always appears in books on preservation and, because the home-made version is so popular, it would be remiss of me not to include it.

Lemon curd is, in its simplest form, a sweetened egg-and-lemon sauce which has thickened through heat. It has poor keeping qualities and should always be stored in the refrigerator, and then only for two or three weeks. Commercial varieties, with permitted preservatives, remain fresher longer and, unless stated on the jar, do not require refrigeration.

Lemon Curd
Makes just over 1kg (2lb).

Finely grated peel and juice of 4 large lemons
125g (4oz) butter
3 large eggs + 1 yolk, beaten well together
350g (12oz) granulated sugar

1 Put all the ingredients into the top of a double saucepan or into a basin standing over a saucepan of gently boiling water.
2 Cook, stirring almost non-stop, until curd thickens sufficiently to coat the back of a spoon.
3 *Do not allow to boil* or the curd may separate and look like sour milk or a curdled mayonnaise.
4 Pour into clean, dry and warm jars and store as for jam.
5 Refrigerate when cold.

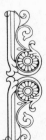

Fruit cheeses have long been family favourites, and most grand-mothers had their own versions.

Damson Cheese
Gather the fruit when full ripe, and to every peck of damsons allow four pounds of lump sugar. Set the fruit in an oven and let it remain until soft; when cold, rub it through a colander or coarse hair-sieve; then put it into a preserving-pan and boil it quickly half an hour; after which add the sugar and kernels, and boil together half an hour longer, stirring it all the time. Wet the moulds with brandy or vinegar. When cold, put the cheese into them. Put on a paper dipped in vinegar, and keep them in a dry place.

Apricot Cheese
Weigh an equal quantity of pared fruit and sugar, wet the latter a very little, and let it boil quickly, or the colour will be spoiled; blanch the kernels, and add to it. Twenty or thirty minutes will boil it. Put it in small pots or cups half filled.

From J. H. Walsh, *Domestic Economy* (c 1877)

Here is a definition and a recipe for Fruit Paste, which was very similar to today's Fruit Cheese:

Of Fruit Pastes

Pastes are fruits of which the pulp has been extracted, reduced into paste by heat, and being mixed with sugar, become of a consistence susceptible of taking any shape you please.

Apple Paste

Take apples, according to the quantity of paste you wish to make, boil them in water till they are quite soft, then take them out of the water, mash and pass them through a hair sieve; weigh the pulp and put it into a pan. Take the same weight of sugar, clarify it, and boil it to the *large feather;* take it off, mix it with the pulp, then put it on a slow fire, and stir it with a spaddle; when it begins to boil a little, it is done; pour it out thin on plates, or in moulds, which must be previously placed on sheets of tin: they may be of different shapes, as hearts, circles, &c. That which you run out on plates, after remaining twenty-four hours in the stove, may be cut in rings, or fillets to form knots, or any other form you please.

Apricot Paste

Take ripe apricots, put them into boiling water, boil them two or three minutes to soften them, and pass them through a hair sieve ; put back the pulp into the pan to reduce it, stirring it with a spaddle lest it should burn to the bottom; when brought to a pulpy consistence, take it from the fire, weigh it, and to every pound of pulp put half a pound of loaf-sugar, clarify it, and boil it to a *feather;* add the pulp, put it back on the fire to boil for a minute, and when you find your paste drop off easily from the spaddle, take it from the fire, fill your moulds, and dry it as before ; or you may make papers plaited on pieces of wood, to the required shape, and fill and dry them in the stove in the same way; when dry, you must wet the papers to take out the paste.

From W. A. Jarrin, *The Italian Confectioner* (c 1861)

8
Fruit Syrups

In a sense, fruit syrups are a kind of simplified and liquid version of fruit jellies. They make the most superb drinks when mixed with soda water and ice in the summer, or added to hot toddies in the winter. The syrups also make excellent milk shakes: but to prevent curdling, it is important to add the syrup to the milk and not the other way round. In cooking, fruit syrups can be used in sorbets, mousses, trifles and jellies.

Choice of Fruits

Choose black- or redcurrants, loganberries and raspberries, mulberries if available, strawberries, blackberries, gooseberries and whortleberries. Check fruits carefully and discard any which are mildewed or obviously over-ripe. The best syrups are made with fruits which have just become ripe. For added flavour interest, use a mixture of two or three fruits.

Water

Add *no water* at all to most fruits. But add 275ml ($\frac{1}{2}$pt) water to $\frac{1}{2}$kg (1lb) blackcurrants, and add 275ml ($\frac{1}{2}$pt) water to $3\frac{1}{2}$kg (6lb) blackberries.

There are two methods of making syrups:

Method 1
(This method prevents fruit from over-cooking.)
1 Put fruit – or fruit and water as directed above – into a basin standing over a pan of gently boiling water.
2 Leave about 1 hour for every $3\frac{1}{2}$kg (6lb) fruit, or until juice begins to run freely. Crush fruit periodically with the back of a wooden spoon or stainless-steel fork to speed up the process and extract as much juice as possible.
3 Crush once more, then strain through a scalded jelly bag or scalded cloth. Allow juice to drip directly into bowl, then measure off in 575 and 275ml (1 and $\frac{1}{2}$pt) amounts.

Method 2
1 Place fruit (and water if used) in saucepan.
2 Stand pan over low heat and crush fruit as much as possible.
3 Bring to the boil and boil 1 minute.
4 Crush fruit again, then strain through a scalded jelly bag or scalded cloth. Allow the juice to drip directly into a bowl, then measure off into 575 and 275ml (1 and $\frac{1}{2}$pt) batches.

Note: Instead of straining the pulp through a jelly bag, an electric juice extractor can be used.

Sugar

Next, add the sugar. Allow 350g (12oz) caster or preserving sugar to every 575ml (1pt) fruit juice. Put both into the saucepan and dissolve over a very low heat, stirring almost constantly. Strain once more through a scalded jelly bag or scalded cloth.

Bottling the Syrup

Pour fruit syrup into screw-topped bottles (such as well-cleaned glass ketchup or sauce bottles), leaving 2½cm (1in) headroom.

Processing

Screw on tops (which must be very clean) then loosen slightly by about one quarter turn. Stand bottles in a *deep* pan of cold water with a false bottom or, as a substitute, several thicknesses of old newspaper. The water should come to within 2½cm (1in) of the tops of the bottles. Bring the water slowly up to simmering point and continue to simmer for 20 minutes. Carefully remove bottles, stand them on a cloth or newspaper and tighten screw tops. Label.

Storage

Store as jam but check frequently for deterioration. Once opened and left at room temperature, the syrups should be used up within 2–3 days; within 10 days if opened and left in the refrigerator.

Lemon or Orange Syrups

These have a superbly fresh flavour and are well worth making when citrus fruits are at their cheapest, usually in the winter. The syrups may be diluted by adding 5 or 6 parts of water or soda water to 1 part of syrup. Store no longer than two months, otherwise both the flavour and colour will show signs of deterioration.

For Lemon Syrup use . . .
Finely grated peel of 6 washed and dried lemons
⅞ litre (1½pt) water
1kg (2lb) + 75g (6oz) granulated sugar
575ml (1pt) strained lemon juice (10–16 lemons depending on size)
8g (¼oz) citric acid (available from pharmacies)

For Orange Syrup use . . .
Finely grated peel of 4 washed and dried oranges
575ml (1pt) strained orange juice (about 8 oranges, depending on size)
1kg (2lb) + 175g (6oz) granulated sugar

Method for Lemon and Orange Syrups
1 Put grated peel into pan with water and sugar.
2 Stir over low heat until sugar dissolves.
3 Strain. Add lemon and citric acid or orange juice.
4 Pour into screw-topped sauce or ketchup bottles.
5 Process as given for fruit syrups.

Note: Instead of processing lemon and orange syrups by heating, they can be preserved with sulphur dioxide, better known in the world of preservation as Camden tablets. Add one tablet, first dissolved in 1 tablespoon warm water, to every 575ml (1pt) syrup. Pour into well-stoppered bottles and store as directed for other fruit syrups. Read section on 'Bottling Fruit with Chemicals', but note that it is *not necessary* to boil syrup before use as the amount of sulphur in the diluted syrup is very small and therefore tasteless.

All fruit syrups may be frozen like herbs – poured into ice-cube trays fitted with dividers, and left until hard. They can then be transferred to polythene bags and used as required.

Our preference for 'natural' foods goes back further than we sometimes realise.

Fruit Syrups

Syrups made from the juices of fresh, ripe fruits are much more troublesome to prepare than those made from essences, and, in consequence, are more seldom used; but for superiority of flavour the essence is not to be compared with the natural fruit syrup.

Lemon Syrup

One pint plain syrup, half teaspoonful (about) soluble essence of lemon, quarter ounce of citric acid. Mix and drink with water or soda water. Ginger, pineapple, sarsaparilla and other extracts are made from the same formula. The recipes may be varied to suit individual tastes, but in all cases where essences are used colouring must be added to resemble as closely as possible the natural colour of the fruit. It is highly important that only soluble and concentrated oils should be used. A cheap essence is poor economy, for it is not only wanting in flavour and strength, but many of the mixtures are positively harmful in quality. Tinctures which are not soluble do not mix well with water— and, especially in the case of lemon, orange, ginger, cloves, cinnamon and peppermint—they impart an objectionable, medicated, oily flavour to the syrup.

From Mary Pope, *Novel Dishes for Vegetarian Households* (c 1893)

Syrup of Pinks

½ lb of Pinks, 1 lb of Sugar.

Pick off all the green parts from half a pound of pinks, put the flowers in a mortar, and pound them with a pint of boiling water; strain the decoction through a cloth; clarify one pound of loaf-sugar (see No. 2), boil it to a *ball* (see No. 10), and add it to the decoction; put it again on the fire, and boil it to a *pearl* (see No. 7). This syrup may also be made without pounding the flowers, only boiling them with the sugar; when done, skim it, and strain it through a cloth. The dark-red velvety single-pink is the best for syrup.

Violet Syrup

Is made in the same way as the preceding, only leaving the flowers half a day in boiling water, in a close and very warm place. The *garden* violet, of a dark colour, is the best for the confectioner, as its perfume is the strongest, and does not escape so soon in working. Syrup of roses is made the same as violet syrup.

From W. A. Jarrin, *The Italian Confectioner* (c 1861)

9
Jam

Jam is a natural sweet preserve made by boiling together fruit – or a combination of fruits – with water and sugar, until the mixture forms a characteristic and spreadable gel. It is probably the most eagerly made and widely used method of fruit preservation and, like honey, is common to most countries of the world.

It is not difficult to account for its popularity. Fruit of some kind grows almost everywhere, both wild and cultivated, and so do edible berries such as rosehips. Sugar is readily available and comparatively inexpensive. The equipment necessary for jam-making is basic and therefore easy to come by. Large or small quantities can be prepared at will.

Once potted, jam stores well, provided certain elementary precautions are taken. It matures on keeping and if properly made, deterioration is minimal. It is versatile in use and is one of the best and most economical ways of utilising surplus fruit. Moreover, jam-making techniques are easy to learn and if the elementary principles are followed, there is no reason for home-made jam to be anything but excellent in texture, colour and flavour.

The Fruit

The most important ingredient is, obviously, the fruit and the best results are achieved when it is slightly under-ripe, still firm and absolutely dry. However, a mixture of ripe and under-ripe fruit is acceptable and produces perfectly satisfactory jam. What should always be avoided is over-ripe fruit which is wet, in part mildewed, and generally in poor condition as the jam will be of inferior quality, will not set properly and will have a short shelf life.

Pectin and Acid

Two things are responsible for making jam set properly when combined with the correct proportion of sugar and water where called for. One is a gum or gel-like substance called pectin, which is found in the cells of fruits, and the other is acid.

Both pectin and acid are present in all fruits but the amounts vary considerably from one type to another, and this is why the kind of bygone-days measurements of ½kg (1lb) fruit to ½kg (1lb) sugar, often found in older cookery books, are altogether misleading and inaccurate.

The proportion of fruit to sugar and water varies significantly and, as you will see under individual entries later in the book, very much depends on the variety of fruit selected. For example, when a fruit is rich both in pectin and acid (like blackcurrants), 350g (12oz) will easily set ½kg (1lb) sugar. If, however, equal quantities were to be used, the jam would become stiff, rubbery and not as palatable as it should be.

Conversely, if double the amount of rhubarb, characteristically low in pectin, were used, it would still be unlikely to set ½kg (1lb) sugar, and the jam would turn out thin and syrupy with uncertain keeping qualities.

Fruits strong in pectin and acid

Just as it is an established fact that wet fruit is deficient in pectin and acid and therefore makes poor jam, so it has been proved by long and careful research that strong fruits (those which are abundant both in pectin and acid) make excellent jam with a long shelf-life. Fruits in this category are cooking and crab apples, all varieties of currants, cooking plums, damsons, gooseberries, fruit from the Japonica tree, quinces (provided they are combined with acid) and wild berries which grow in the uplands and lowlands of the British Isles and are known by different names from north to south.

Medium-strong fruits

Medium-strong fruits, where a good set can be expected from a proportion of $\frac{3}{4}$kg (1lb) fruit to $\frac{1}{2}$kg (1lb) sugar, include greengages, very fresh blackberries, under-ripe apricots, mulberries, sloes, raspberries and loganberries.

Weak fruits

Weak fruits, all lowish in acid and with varying amounts of pectin, are dessert apples, dessert pears, cherries, most types of strawberries, Morello cherries, elderberries, rhubarb, medlars, melon, marrow and ageing blackberries.

To achieve a good balance and subsequently a good set, it is sensible to combine a strong or medium fruit with a weak one. Typical combinations are apple and blackberry, rhubarb and redcurrant, and gooseberries with dessert cherries.

If a mixture of fruit is disliked or for some reason considered unsuitable, commercial pectin (such as Certo) may be added to a weak fruit or a vegetable jam such as marrow. What I must stress here though is that directions on the jar or bottle must be followed very carefully, as recipes have been worked out with the utmost care by the manufacturer and any deviation could mean failure.

Should the instructions be unclear, add 50–125ml (2–4oz) liquid pectin or 8g ($\frac{1}{4}$oz) powdered pectin to every $\frac{1}{2}$kg (1lb) of weak fruit such as rhubarb, dessert cherries and melon. If too much pectin is added, the flavour and colour of the jam may be spoiled.

Acid, where required, should be added to the fruit at the *beginning* of cooking, as it aids the extraction of pectin and helps to ensure a firm set. To every 2kg (4lb) fruit, use either 2 tablespoons lemon juice or $\frac{1}{2}$ level teaspoon citric or tartaric acid (available from pharmacies). If preferred, although it is somewhat more bothersome, simmer $\frac{1}{2}$kg (1lb) gooseberries, redcurrants or cut up and unpeeled cooking apples in 275ml ($\frac{1}{2}$pt) water in a covered pan. When very soft, strain through a fine mesh sieve or cloth jelly bag and add 150ml ($\frac{1}{4}$pt) juice to every 2kg (4lb) fruit.

Sugar

Cube and preserving sugar create less scum than any other and therefore produce clearer jam with a greater degree of sparkle (important for competitions). However, as granulated sugar is less expensive, it is probably a natural choice for economy reasons alone. But what must be borne in mind is that you may be called upon to skim the jam more frequently which can be bothersome and tiring – and also waste more of it because every time you skim away the surface layer, inevitably you take with it a certain amount of jam. For this reason, many authorities recommend skimming once only, at the very end and after the jam has reached setting point.

Here initiative has to come in and if the jam is excessively foamy, then obviously it will need skimming more than once. The cook has to decide. The buildup of scum can be lessened, and so can burning, if the inside of the preserving pan is brushed with a layer of melted butter, margarine or glycerine before jam making begins. Alternatively, a knob of butter stirred into the jam after it has reached setting point helps to disperse some of the scum, though a certain amount may still cling round the edges and skimming will therefore be necessary.

It is advisable to warm the sugar (either in the oven or briefly in a microwave) before adding it to the fruit and water. The reasons are well-founded: warm sugar dissolves much more quickly than cold, cools down the mixture less and, a consideration these days, saves cooking fuel.

In general, because sugar has a toughening effect on fruit it is added to the fruit and water when the mixture has cooked down to a soft and pulpy mass and any skins have totally tenderised. But there are exceptions. If the appearance of the jam is improved by whole fruit or pieces of fruit (strawberries for example), then the sugar is sprinkled over the uncooked fruit and left to stand overnight. Because of sugar's toughening effect, the fruit will stay firm instead of disintegrating into a pulp when cooked.

Water

The amounts used will depend on the fruit and, whereas fruits juicy and soft by nature, such as raspberries and strawberries, may require no water at all, others like black-currants need to be simmered in a com-paratively large amount: about $1\frac{3}{4}$ litres (3pt) to every 2kg (4lb) fruit. Be guided by individual entries later in the book.

Equipment

You will need a large pan with a sturdy base. It may be made of stainless steel (copper-based for preference), aluminium or heavy and *unchipped* enamel.

Alternatively, old-fashioned copper pre-serving pans can be used with absolute peace of mind. They are not in any way dangerous – as some people seem to think – and in some instances the greenish tinge from the metal actually improves the colour of the jam. Bad choices are unlined or galvanised iron, as acid from the fruit erodes and eats into the metal and also spoils the flavour and colour of the jam.

A long-handled wooden spoon is necessary for stirring (not metal because it becomes too hot to hold comfortably), and so is a plate near the pan where you can lay the spoon in between stirring.

When it comes to test for setting, a few clean saucers are useful to have around and, for very accurate results, a sugar or pre-serving thermometer (not the medical type) is useful: well worth buying if you happen to be keen, long-term, on making your own preserves in quantity.

Please remember that jam foams up in the pan and to avoid boiling over, the danger of burning, and a messy cooker, the pan should be no more than half-full after the sugar has been added. Personally, I prefer to make jam in small quantities – several batches instead of one big one – because the operation runs more smoothly and quickly and there is less risk of overcooking and spoiling the flavour and colour of the fruit.

Making the Jam

Proportions for individual jams are given later in the book, in the entries for individual fruits, but as a general rule simmer the fruit in the water long and slowly until it has completely softened (currants can take up to one hour's simmering) *before* adding the sugar.

Once the sugar has been added to the pan, stir it round with the fruit and water until every particle has dissolved. Increase heat and boil jam *briskly* until setting point has been reached.

Two important factors to remember: keep the lid on the pan when fruit is simmering, off the pan after the sugar has been added; stir occasionally to prevent sticking.

To Test for Setting

There are several methods, some rather technical and best carried out under laboratory conditions. For general home purposes, the following three tests are the most manageable and should be tried about 3–5 minutes after the jam has been brought to a brisk and rolling boil.

1 Pour a *little* jam on to a *cold* saucer and leave for 2 minutes. If a skin forms on top which crinkles up when you touch it, then setting point has been reached. As soon as you have poured the jam on to the saucer, take the pan off the heat, otherwise boiling will automatically continue and overcooking could result.

2 Dip the wooden spoon deep down into the jam, lift it up and hold it horizontally over the pan. Watch the edge. If the drops of jam partially set, gather together in little dollops and break slowly but cleanly away from the spoon, setting point has been reached.

3 Rinse a sugar or preserving thermometer in hot water. Stand it vertically in the pan of well-stirred jam, making sure the bulb is not in direct contact with the base of the pan. Setting point is reached when the temperature registers 104°C (220°F), although a marginally firmer set may be achieved at 105°C (221/2°F).

Potting the Jam

When setting point has been reached, the pan should be removed from the heat and the jam skimmed with a perforated spoon washed in hot water and then dried.

The jam should then be ladled into clean, bone-dry and warm glass or pottery jars of either ½ or 1kg (1 or 2lb) capacity. Smaller containers may be used if preferred but irrespective of size or type, it is essential that the jam reaches right to the top of the jars to allow for the substantial shrinkage which generally occurs on cooling.

If the jam contains whole pieces of fruit, as in the case of strawberries, the jam should be left in the pan in which it was cooked until a skin forms on top. Afterwards, it should be stirred gently round and potted as described previously. If it was ladled into jars immediately, the fruit would rise to the top instead of being suspended all through the gel-like syrup.

Waxed discs, of an exact fit, should be pressed gently on top of the jam in each container while it is still very hot. The discs, waxed sides down, should be placed directly on the jam to prevent mould from developing and must be neither so small that rings of jam are left unprotected round the outside edges, nor so large that the discs form protruding frills round the tops of the jars.

Once the jam is completely cold, the rims of the jars should be wiped clean and then the jars covered with cellophane circles held in place with elastic bands. If preferred or more convenient, parchment may be used as an alternative to cellophane.

Every jar of jam should be labelled clearly with variety and date.

Storage

A dry, cool and well-ventilated cupboard is the ideal storage place for jam. What it dislikes and reacts against are dampness, which encourages mould, and a warm and moist atmosphere which causes shrinkage.

Jam made from Frozen Fruits

When fruit is frozen, the pectin within the cells loses some of its power and this applies particularly to strawberries and other soft fruits. Therefore add either an extra 225g (8oz) of fruit to every 2½kg (5lb) sugar – keeping the proportion of sugar and water the same – or use commercial pectin.

You can, if preferred, add 225g (8oz) fresh gooseberries or redcurrants to every 2½kg (5lb) frozen fruit.

It is worth knowing that if blackcurrants are going to be frozen for the prime purpose of jam-making, they should be blanched in boiling water for one minute, cooled completely and then packaged for freezing.

Light-coloured fruits – which should, by rights, remain light-coloured – often darken during cooking. One way round the problem is to coat the fruit in sugar prior to freezing, and the proportion is ½kg (1lb) to every 2½kg (5lb) fruit. When the fruit is being made into jam, it is important to remember to *decrease* proportionately the amount of sugar in the recipe.

Freezer Jams

Freezer jams are delectable preserves with an incredibly rotund, fruity flavour, exquisite bouquet and vividness of colour that distinguishes them from all other jams. Basically they are made from uncooked fruit which is first crushed or mashed and mixed with acid and sugar. This mixture is then left to stand for about ½ hour before liquid pectin (any of the standard commercial varieties) is added. The jam is again left for another 5 minutes, stirred round and transferred to small and scrupulously clean plastic pots. After covering with lids (but leaving 1¼cm or ½in headroom for expansion), it must be allowed to settle and set at kitchen temperature for about 5 to 6 hours before being placed in the refrigerator until it gels; a process which should take between 24 and 48 hours. The pots should finally be stored in the freezer for up to 6 months.

To thaw, leave at kitchen temperature between 1 and 2 hours. Stir round and serve, or use as required. Once open, the jams should be covered and left in the refrigerator up to 3 days – no longer, because they do not store well out of the freezer.

A Reminder – Fruit and Pectin

The basic proportion of fruit to pectin remains the same irrespective of type and kind of fruit being used – 550g (1¼lb) to 125ml (4 fl oz) liquid pectin. What does vary is the amount of sugar and acid which have to be added, so please be guided by individual entries later in the book.

Faults and their Causes

Fermentation – insufficient sugar used, and/or underboiled.

Crystallisation – too much sugar used, and/or insufficient acid.

Dull colour – jam cooked too long after sugar was added. Jam lacked acid.

Tough skins – fruit and sugar insufficiently cooked before sugar was added.

Jam runny – fruit lacked acid or pectin or both. Fruit over-ripe. Fruit underboiled. Too much sugar.

Jam stiff and rubbery – Proportions incorrect. Insufficient sugar and water used for the amount of fruit.

Mouldy – insecurely covered. Stored in damp conditions.

Sticky – overcooked.

Too dark – overcooked.

Flavour spoiled – overcooked.

Our children today may not thank us for a jam which 'is better than nothing', but in fact Victorian and Edwardian cooks made splendid jams.

Carrot Jam

Boil some carrots till quite tender, and rub them through a sieve. To one pound of the pulp add three-quarters of a pound of loaf sugar; boil it to a jam, and when nearly cold add the juice and grated rind of two lemons, and half a teaspoonful of essence of cloves or nutmegs. This jam is not very good, as compared with some others, but for children it is better than nothing, and very wholesome.

Mixed Preserve for Children

Take raspberries, red currants and white currants, in any quantities which are left, or gooseberries and black currants in equal quantities; boil them together for twenty minutes or half an hour, according to their weight; then common moist sugar, dried and heated before the fire, must be added in the proportion of three-quarters of a pound to each pound of fruit, and boiled five minutes longer.

From J. H. Walsh, *Domestic Economy* (c 1877)

Blackberry and Plum Jam

Open the plums and crack the stones. Let there be 1 lb. of plums to 3 of blackberries; see that the blackberries have been gathered during dry weather. Put all into a large saucepan and boil for one hour, skim well and carefully. Then add six pounds of sugar to every seven pounds of fruit; boil it for half or three quarters of an hour, fill the jars, and when it is cold, tie down. Blackberry and apple jam, or plain blackberry, may be made as above, leaving out the plums and substituting peeled, cored, and sliced apples, or by boiling the berries by themselves.

From *Hughes's Domestic Economy* (c 1892)

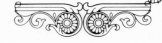

Cherry Jam

2 lbs. of Cherries, 1 lb. of Sugar.

Choose two pounds of very ripe cherries, of a fine colour, take out the stones and stalks, put them into a pan on the fire, and reduce them nearly one half. Clarify two pounds of loaf-sugar, and boil it to the *little crack;* add the pulp, and mix it in well; put it back on the fire, and stir it with the spaddle: when you can easily see the bottom of the pan, you may be certain of its being done enough.

From W. A. Jarrin, *The Italian Confectioner* (c 1861)

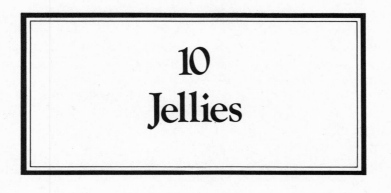

10
Jellies

These are often the star attraction of the whole preserving show: crystal-clear and gleaming versions of jam, made from fruit, sugar and water. Mellow-coloured, exquisitely flavoured and the joy of every good cook's heart!

The making of jellies is very similar to that of jam but more patience is needed, perhaps a little more practice and, speaking personally, more care.

For example, the fruit. This has to be selected with a watchful eye, as it must be fresh, dry and slightly under-ripe. Another important factor is the kind of fruit chosen. Excellent for jellies, again because they are rich both in acid and pectin (see Jam section, page 48), are members of the currant family, quinces, crab apples, cranberries, blackberries, bilberries (sometimes called whortleberries), loganberries, gooseberries, raspberries, damsons, and sour apples on their own or mixed with sloes. Unsuitable fruits, because of their poor setting qualities and/or appearance, are strawberries, cherries, plums, pears, marrows, melons, very ripe apricots and peaches.

Equipment

The equipment for jelly making is much the same as for jam but, in addition, you will need what is commonly called a jelly bag. This is usually made from material such as coarse muslin, linen used for tea-towels (I have, in fact, often improvised with an old tea-towel) or loosely woven white cotton, felt and even flannel. I bought a very smart-looking jelly bag and matching bowl, to catch the juice, in Sweden and I believe similar ones are available over here, but a square cut from any of the materials mentioned above will do perfectly well.

Sew tapes on to each of the four corners, and these can then be tied over the legs of an upturned stool and suspended down the middle. What is essential is to ensure that there is a bowl standing underneath before you start!

On a hygienic note, it is advisable to scald the bag with boiling water at least twice before making the jelly.

Cooking the Fruit

Hard fruits (such as quinces and apples) should be washed and dried, cut up coarsely without peeling, but left uncored or unstoned. Unsound portions must be removed and discarded, as must stalks and leaves. There is no need, either, to hull berry fruits.

Put the fruit into a large pan with water to cover, although tough-skinned fruits – currants and plums for example – will need slightly more water as they take longer to soften and therefore longer to cook. Subsequent and excessive evaporation could result which might ultimately spoil the jelly.

Cook the fruit slowly, with the lid on the pan, for between $\frac{3}{4}$ and 1 hour in order to extract the acid and pectin – again so vital for a satisfactory gel.

Straining

Tip the contents of the pan gently into the prepared bag and allow to drip steadily for about 1 hour or until the process has stopped by itself.

If you squeeze the bag in an attempt to speed things up, particles of fruit will be forced through and the jelly will become cloudy. While this may make no odds for home use, it would be a complete waste of time entering such jellies for competitions, where clarity is an all-important factor.

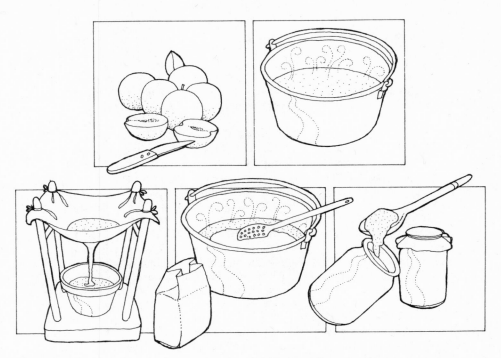

Adding Sugar

Measure the juice and pour it into a preserving pan. The amount of sugar you add will, to some extent, depend on the fruits used. For those that are rich both in acid and pectin (see Jam making section), allow ½kg (1lb) sugar to 575ml (1pt) juice. For weaker fruits (see Jam section), use 350/400g (12/14 oz) sugar to every 575ml (1pt) juice.

Cooking

Bring juice to boil. Add sugar. Leave over medium heat and stir until sugar has completely dissolved. Bring to the boil. Boil briskly and steadily, uncovered, for about 10 minutes before testing for setting. (See Jam making section if you are unsure about this.) Keep pan *uncovered* throughout. For pale-coloured juices – such as apple – add sugar to the cold juice. The longer cooking time deepens and enriches the colour.

Skimming

A knob of butter, stirred in after setting point has been reached, often disperses the scum. Alternatively, run a hot spoon across the surface. To be absolutely sure that no speck of scum remains, strain the still-liquid jelly through a clean jelly bag. You must move fast so that this can be done before the jelly sets, but I have to admit that this final stage is for purists only!

Potting

Pot, cover and store jelly as for jam. To avoid air bubbles as you bottle the jelly, tilt the jar or jars and pour the jelly slowly down the side. Pour slowly and tip each jar up until jelly reaches the brim.

Yield

This is difficult to ascertain accurately, but 2¼kg (5lb) jelly is the usual amount one can expect from 1½kg (3lb) sugar.

Jellies, like jams, have changed little over the years. Red currant jelly has long been a favourite; but we do tend to forget today that mixtures of fruits can work very well.

Red Currant Jelly.

The following is a good receipt for Red Currant jelly, one of the preserves best worth making at home:—Gather the Currants on a dry day. Strip them off their stalks, and squeeze the juice through a cloth. Leave the juice to stand in the cellar for twenty-four hours ; then pour it into another cloth, carefully leaving the thick sediment behind. For each pound of juice allow one pound of powdered white sugar (not bought ready pounded, but done at home). Put the juice on the fire in the preserving-pan, and keep stirring it from the first with a silver spoon, adding the sugar, which should be standing close by, in spoonfuls. When the sugar is all added and dissolved, it will be necessary to take off the rising scum with a flat sieve-spoon, very well scalded and cleaned previously; and by placing a little jelly on a saucer it will be seen by the consistency when it has jellied. As soon as there is a sign of this take the pan off the fire, let it stand five or ten minutes, and fill the jelly glasses, which should previously have been well sulphured, and be standing ready face downwards. Next day they should be covered with rounds of paper soaked in brandy. Half a teaspoonful of brandy should be sprinkled over each glass, and then they should be tied or gummed up in the usual way.

From Mrs. G. W. Earle, *Pot-Pourri From a Surrey Garden* (c 1899)

Four-Fruit Jelly

Take equal quantities of ripe strawberries, raspberries, currants, and red cherries. All should be fully ripe, and the cherries must be stoned, taking care to save the juice that comes from them in stoning. Add it afterwards to the rest. Mix the fruit together, and put it in a linen bag. Squeeze it well into a tureen placed beneath. When it has ceased to drip, measure the juice ; and to every pint, allow a pound and two ounces of the best double-refined loaf sugar, in large lumps. Mix together the juice and the sugar; put them into an enamelled preserving-pan; set it over the fire, and let it boil half an hour—skimming it frequently. Try the jelly by dipping out a spoonful, and holding it in the open air. If it congeals readily, it is sufficiently done. Put the jelly warm into wide-topped glasses. Cover it with double tissue paper, which must be white, and cut exactly to fit the surface of the jelly. Lay it nicely and smoothly inside the top of the glass, pressing it down with the fingers all round the edge. Then tie down with the white-of-egg paper.

From J. H. Walsh, *Domestic Economy* (c 1877)

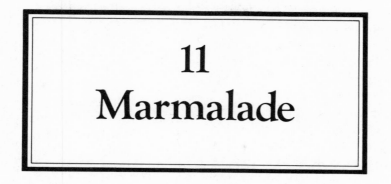

11
Marmalade

Marmalade is basically jam made from citrus fruits, and although considered a particularly English breakfast preserve, most countries where oranges, limes, lemons and grapefruit grow also produce their own versions of citrus preserves. These range from thin or thick jellies for spreading, to pieces or slices of fruits suspended in very sweet syrup: these are rarely, if ever, eaten on bread or toast but are treated more as a luxurious sweetmeat, particularly in places like the Balkans, parts of Southern Europe and the Middle East.

Most of the rules for jam-making apply equally to marmalade, so please turn to the jam section and read through it carefully *before* beginning to tackle marmalades that have their own distinctive characteristics.

Types of Citrus

The most usual fruits to use for marmalades are bitter or Seville oranges (with us during the winter), grapefruit, lemons and the somewhat costly limes. Also used are sweet oranges and members of the tangerine family. For recipes, see under individual fruits.

All fruit must be thoroughly washed and dried before use, and scrubbed if dirty.

Pectin

Most of the pectin contained in citrus fruits is to be found in the pips and pith, and the remainder is in the coarse membranes between the sections of flesh. Thus to ensure a good set, every part of the fruit, including the pips, must be used in cooking, although the pips and pith are usually tied in a piece of thin cloth and not left to float about loosely in the marmalade.

Cutting the Peel

The thickness of the pieces of peel depends very much on personal taste and if thick pieces are preferred, then cut peel, plus pith, into stubby and even lengths. Medium-cut needs no explanation but 'shred' means exactly what it says: remove all traces of pith from the peel, keep it on one side and then cut the peel into thin, thin shreds of even length and thickness. The cutting of peel is always better carried out by hand, because you have greater control over the size of the pieces. However, to save time and effort, you can use the slicing attachment of an electric mixer, the coarse blade of the mincer attachment or a hand-worked shredding machine.

Cooking the Peel

Peel in general (and the thick pieces especially) takes longer to cook than fruit for jam making. Thus more water must be allowed, because of the greater evaporation of liquid which inevitably takes place. Be guided in this by individual entries later in the book, but also remember that it takes longer to extract pectin from thick pieces of peel than it does from thin shreds.

The skins of sweet oranges tend to make cloudy marmalade so do not be dismayed or downhearted if this happens and look up every book on the subject to see where you went wrong. The marmalade may not win a beauty contest but it will be perfectly good to eat and that is all that truly matters for home use. As a matter of interest, the peel of bitter oranges becomes transparent and gives the marmalade an attractive appearance; the peel of other citrus fruits remains opaque.

Acid

As you go through the recipes, you will notice that extra acid – lemon juice, citric acid or tartaric acid – is nearly always included. This may puzzle many people – as it did me at first – because, on the face of it, what could be more acid than sour oranges and grapefruit? Long Ashton's Bulletin No 21 (published by HMSO), called Home Preservation of Fruit and Vegetables, neatly solves the riddle this way:

·Why add more acid when using such acid fruits? The answer is that it is the total amount of acid in relation to the amount of marmalade that is important in securing a good jelly. From ½kg (1lb) of Seville oranges (of which nearly half the weight is in the skins) approximately 1½kg (3lb) marmalade is obtained; it is clear that the acid present in this comparatively small amount of fruit is not enough to give a good set with the pectin and sugar, hence the addition of lemon juice or acid.

In other words, ½kg (1lb) grapefruit, for example, has no more acid than 225g (8oz) plums but is expected to yield twice as much preserve! For amounts of acid to add, be guided by individual entries later in the book.

Cooking the Fruit

Whichever recipe you are using, it is essential to cook the fruit and peel long and slowly initially *before* adding any sugar. This is to extract as much pectin as possible and also to soften the peel. Although specific amounts and proportions of water to fruit are given in the recipes in individual entries, you are usually safe if you allow 1¼ litres (2pt) water to every ½kg (1lb) of fruit if making the marmalade in a preserving or other suitable pan; half the amount of water if making the marmalade in a pressure cooker.

I have mentioned several times that long, slow cooking of the fruit and peel – with the addition of the pips and pith tied in a cloth – is essential for success. Therefore allow between 2 and 2½ hours, and ensure that the peel is soft enough to disintegrate completely when rubbed between finger and thumb. Uncover halfway through the cooking time in order to boil off some of the water and reduce the volume by about one-half.

Soaking the Fruit prior to Cooking

Research has proven that soaking fruit overnight has little beneficial effect on marmalade. However, you can soften the pith a little by soaking it with the pips (both tied up in cloth) in half the specified amount of water overnight.

Adding the Sugar

After the fruit and water have been cooked for the length of time suggested, add the sugar, stir until dissolved, then boil the marmalade *briskly* until setting point is reached: 15–20 minutes. Test for setting as directed under jam, but cook a little longer if marmalade remains runny. *Do not overcook* or colour and flavour will be spoiled.

Methods

There are several methods of making marmalade.

Method 1

1 Wash and scrub fruit and peel as you would for eating.
2 If the peel is very pithy remove some of the pith and reserve. On the other hand, if

you prefer a very thick and chunky marmalade, leave the pith where it is.

3 Cut the peel into strips, the width and length depending on personal taste. It is worth knowing that they swell up a little during cooking. Put into the preserving pan with the additional acid called for in the recipe.

4 Squeeze juice from fruit. Add to pan. Put pips into a piece of cloth. Chop up squeezed pulp, including white pith, and add to pips. Tie up cloth securely to form a bag. Transfer to pan. Add water. Cook about 2–2½ hours or until contents are reduced by half and the peel is very soft.

5 Remove bag of pips etc. Squeeze between two plates, holding directly over pan so that the juices run back into the fruit etc, and none of the pectin is lost.

6 Add sugar. Proceed as for jam.

Method 2

I call this 'the quick one' because the peel and pulp are minced together and there is no tedious slicing – a chore which can be off-putting for those with minimal spare time.

The marmalade is of the coarse-cut variety and tends to be on the cloudy side. But despite these minor failings – if failings is the right word at all – it has a splendid flavour and deliciously thick texture.

1 Wash and dry fruit well, scrubbing it if necessary. Cut each piece of fruit in half and squeeze out the juice. Pour juice into preserving pan.

2 Collect *all* the pips and tie in a piece of cheesecloth. Add to pan with the coarsely minced 'shells' of the squeezed fruit. Stir in extra acid as called for in the recipe.

3 Pour in water. Bring to boil, lower heat, then simmer slowly for 2–2½ hours or until

contents are reduced by half and the peel is very soft.

4 Continue as directed in points 5 and 6 of Method 1.

Method 3

Cooking the fruit whole, on the cooker or in the oven, has always been popular and is particularly recommended if using frozen fruit.

1 For the oven method (ideal if you have a continuous-burning oven), place well-washed citrus into a large, flameproof casserole. Add recommended amount of water. Cover. Cook 4–5 hours – or until fruit is very tender – in a cool oven set to 150°C (300°F), Gas 2.

2 To simmer on top of the cooker, place fruit in a saucepan. Add recommended amount of water. Cover. Cook gently 2–2½ hours or until contents are reduced by half and fruit is very tender.

3 Take fruit out of casserole or pan and put on to a large plate. Cut up into small pieces using a knife and fork (it will be too hot to hold).

4 Collect all the pips, tie them in a piece of clean cloth and add to liquid in casserole or pan. Boil briskly, uncovered, for ¼ hour which has the effect of extracting as much pectin as possible and also reducing the liquid. Strain pips between two plates held directly over the pan so that the juices are caught and none of the pectin is lost either.

5 Add cut-up fruit, acid and sugar. Stir over moderate heat until sugar dissolves. Bring to boil. Boil briskly until setting point is reached. (Test for this as described in the Jam section.)

Method 4

This again involves cooking fruit on top of the cooker, but for speed and convenience it is carried out in a pressure cooker.

1 Wash and dry about ¾kg (1½lb) fruit. Do not cut. Put into pressure cooker, first removing rack. Add *half* the water recommended in the recipe, which should work out at 575ml (1pt) to every ½kg (1lb) fruit.

2 Put on lid, leaving vent open. Bring slowly to boil. As soon as you can see steam coming out of the vent, close and bring up to 7kg (15lb) pressure.

3 Keep at this pressure for 20 minutes, remove from heat and leave to stand for 10 minutes. Cool down completely then take off lid.

4 Continue as directed from point 3 in Method 3.

Finishing off the Marmalade

Skim almost immediately, otherwise the scum gets very tacky, sticks to the peel obstinately and is tricky to remove.

To prevent peel from rising in the jars – and this is a common fault – leave marmalade in the pan in which it was cooked until it has cooled and a thinnish skin has formed completely over the surface. Stir round gently. Pot and cover as for jam.

Jelly Marmalade – yields 2¼kg (5lb)

I would suggest you read the section on Jelly making *before* trying out the jelly marmalade given below.

1kg (2lb) Seville oranges
Juice of 2 large lemons or 2 level teaspoons citric or tartaric acid (available from pharmacies)
2¾ litres (4½pt) water
1½kg (3lb) granulated, cube or preserving sugar

Method

1 Peel *half* the fruit thinly, removing all traces of pith. (*Do not* throw away). Cut peel into very fine – really fine – shreds.

2 Chop up rest of fruit, with peel and pith, coarsely. Put into pan with pips. Add lemon juice or acid as recommended in the recipe. Also 1½ litres (2½pt) water.

3 Bring to boil. Lower heat. Cover pan. Simmer 2 hours. Meanwhile, gently cook shreds of peel separately in 575ml (1pt) water for 1½ hours. Keep pan covered throughout.

4 Strain peel and reserve. Add liquid from peel to first pan containing fruit, etc. Mix well. Drip through a jelly bag into suitable container for 20 minutes. Do not squeeze the bag at all, or the jelly will be cloudy.

5 Take pulp out of jelly bag. Return to pan. Add remaining water. Boil briskly, uncovered, ½ hour. Once more drip mixture through jelly bag directly into the container holding the first batch of strained liquid.

6 Transfer to pan. Add peel and sugar. Stir over low heat until sugar dissolves. Boil rapidly, uncovered, until setting point is reached, testing as directed in section on jam.

Common Faults in Marmalade Making

Peel tough – peel insufficiently cooked before sugar was added.

Poor set – marmalade lacked acid, or acid was added too late.

Flavour and colour uncharacteristic – contents not reduced by half before sugar was added. Marmalade cooked for too long after sugar was added.

Crystallisation occurs – excess sugar used. Sugar not completely dissolved before marmalade was brought to boil.

Peel rises – marmalade potted while very hot and before a skin formed on surface in preserving pan.

Jelly marmalade 'bubbly' – left for too long before being potted.

'Marmalade' used not necessarily to signify the citrus-fruit preserves we assume today.

Ripe Apricot Marmalade
1 lb. of Apricot Pulp, 1 lb. of Sugar.

Take ripe apricots, put them into boiling water, leave them a few minutes, then take them out, and extract the stones, and pass them through a hair sieve; weigh the pulp, and to every pound take a pound of loaf-sugar; clarify it, boil it to the *great feather;* add your pulp, stirring and boiling it till it hangs on the spaddle like a jelly; take it from the fire, and add the kernels of the apricots which you use, previously blanched and dried.

From W. A. Jarrin, *The Italian Confectioner* (c 1861)

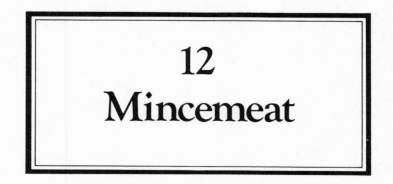

12
Mincemeat

This is in a world of its own and although many moons ago it was based on raw minced beef, the mincemeat we use these days for mince pies and tarts is a spicy, typically British concoction made with dried and fresh fruits, suet, sugar, nuts and frequently alcohol. It has good keeping qualities and the best apples to use are hard dessert ones; Bramleys, with their excessive juiciness, could make the mincemeat wet and slushy.

Mincemeat
Makes about 3½kg (7½lb):

½kg (1lb) apples (peeled and cored weight)
125g (4oz) almonds, blanched
1½kg (3lb) mixed dried fruit to include seedless raisins, sultanas, stoned dates and currants
225g (8oz) chopped mixed peel
½kg (1lb) finely shredded suet
½kg (1lb) soft brown sugar (dark variety)
2 to 3 level teaspoons mixed spice
150ml (¼pt) brandy or whisky

1 Coarsely mince apples with almonds, raisins, sultanas and dates.
2 Stir in rest of ingredients.
3 When well mixed and evenly combined, transfer to jars which should be clean, dry and warm. Cover as for jam.
4 Store in a dry and well-ventilated larder or pantry. Alternatively, keep under refrigeration.

'Mincemeat' used to be just that, a minced meat preparation. But the Soyer recipe below combines meat with dried fruit, perhaps being a halfway stage towards today's Christmas mincemeat.

Mincemeat
Take four cups of suet, two of currants, four of stoned raisins, half a cup of preserved ginger, half a cup of dried citron, a cup of pounded sugar-candy, a grated nutmeg, a dessertspoonful of pounded mace, another of pounded cloves, six wineglassfuls of brandy, and three of noyeau. Mix well.

Mincemeat à la Soyer
Take four pounds and a half of kidney beef suet, which skin and chop very finely; have also a quarter of a pound of candied lemon and orange-peel, the same of citron, a pound and a half of lean cooked beef, and three pounds and a half of apples, the whole separately chopped very fine, and put into a large pan with four pounds and a half of currants well washed and picked, two ounces of mixed spice, and two pounds of sugar. Mix the whole well together with the juice of eight lemons and a pint of brandy, place it in jars, and tie down until ready for use; a pound and a half of Malaga raisins, well stoned and chopped, may likewise be added to the above. It is ready for use in a few days.

From *The Practical Housewife* by the Editor of *The Family Friend* (c 1880)

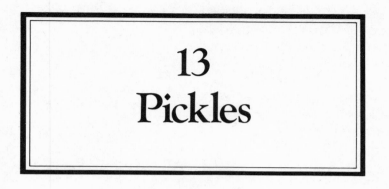

13
Pickles

Pickling is a means of preserving brined vegetables in acid – usually vinegar enhanced with a melange of spices. The end result is pickles: assorted crisp vegetables which are tangy and piquant and, like chutneys, are superb team-mates with all manner of cold foods, from sausages and meat pies to mixed meats and assorted cheeses.

Three things are essential to success
1 Vegetables in prime condition.
2 Brine.
3 Spiced vinegar.

Spiced Vinegar

As this takes somewhere in the region of 8 weeks to make, I shall deal with this first.
1 Put 2½ litres (4pt) vinegar into a large jar or crock. For light vegetables such as small silverskinned onions, cauliflower florets and cucumber, use distilled vinegar, which is colourless. For larger pickling onions, walnuts, beetroots, etc, malt vinegar is adequate.
2 Add 2 level tablespoons pickling spice, 1 cinnamon stick, 1 large and crumbled bay leaf, 1 blade mace or a few grindings of nutmeg and 24 cloves.
3 Cover with thick brown paper then over-wrap with cling film. Leave to stand up to 8 weeks, lifting cover and stirring from time to time. Strain before use.

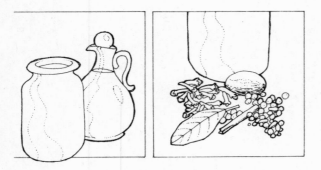

Brine

This is a mixture of salt and water, and the proportion for pickles is ½kg (1lb) kitchen salt to 4¾ litres (8pt) water. To make, add salt to water and leave until dissolved, stirring periodically.

Vegetables

The most popular are onions and/or shallots, cauliflower, beetroot, gherkins, cucumbers, walnuts (which turn jet-black), red cabbage and a combination of mixed vegetables to include cauliflower, onions, French beans and cucumber. Each vegetable has to be treated somewhat differently, so I would ask you to be guided by instructions given under the individual entries later in this book.

Treatment of Brined Vegetables

After placing vegetables in brine, keep them immersed in the solution by covering with a plate weighed down by a couple of bricks or heavy garden stones.

After removing from brine, drain thoroughly and rinse under cold running water. Rinse thoroughly again. The object of brining is to extract some of the moisture from the vegetables, which in turn helps to keep them firm and relatively crisp.

Bottling

After rinsing, the vegetables should be packed into jars to within 2½cm (1in) of the top. Afterwards the jars should be filled with spiced vinegar to within 1¼cm (½in) of the top.

Covering

The best covering is Porosan Skin as it is totally non-corrosive and also prevents evaporation of vinegar. You can successfully use a covering made from three or four thicknesses of cling film, secured with elastic bands, and plastic lids are also very satisfactory. I advise against covering pickles as you would jam, because the wax discs and cellophane tops are too flimsy to prevent evaporation.

Storage

Pickles should be stored in a dark, dry and cool place to prevent discolouration, limpness of vegetables and evaporation of vinegar.

After reading W. G. Lewis's introduction to his section on pickles, one wonders why he pursued the subject . . .

Pickles

Like Dr. Kitchiner, we are not fond of pickles. They are, indeed, for the most part, mere vehicles for taking up vinegar and spice — and very unwholesome, indigestible vehicles they are. By pounding them, as they do in India, they are rendered less indigestible. Those who are fond of relishes, and who are wise enough not to gratify their tastes at the expense of their stomachs, will find the various flavoured vinegars, mixed to each individual's liking, an excellent substitute for pickles.

From W. G. Lewis, *The Cook* (19th century)

Mixed Pickles

Take some small cucumbers, French beans, sprigs of cauliflower, and some white onions. Make a pickle of salt and water that will carry an egg; pour it over them, let them lie for two or three days; then put some cabbage leaves in the bottom of a brass pan, put in the pickles and the salt and water, put it on the fire, let them get hot, but not to boil. Keep them by the side of the fire, or on a slow hot-plate, until they get quite yellow; take them out, and clean out the pan; put some fresh cabbage leaves in the bottom; lay in the pickles, put in an equal quantity of vinegar and water to cover them; shake a handful of salt over them, and cover them with a few cabbage leaves. Set them upon the fire, put on a cover when they become hot, draw them aside, and keep them hot, until they are all green over. Then put them in a sieve to drain; have some vinegar boiled with sliced ginger, a few blades of mace, mustard seeds, and pepper-corn. Put the pickles into bottles or a jar, pour the boiling vinegar over them until they are completely covered, cork and seal them immediately.

From *Pears' Shilling Encyclopaedia* (c 1898)

Pickled Cabbage.

Average cost of "*Pickled Cabbage.*"

INGREDIENTS.

	s.	d.
A red cabbage.............................	0	3
A gallon of vinegar.......................	1	4
Mace, cloves, allspice, whole pepper	0	1½
Salt and ginger	0	0½
	1	9

Time required, about three days.

Now we will show you how to *Pickle a Cabbage*.

1. We take a *red cabbage*, cut it in half, and cut out the *stalk*, and wash it well in *salt* and *cold water*.

> N.B.—A *white-heart cabbage* will do to pickle, but *green cabbages* cannot be used.

2. We put it on a board, and cut it in thin slices.

3. We lay the *slices* in a large pan, sprinkle a *handful of salt* over each layer of *slices*, cover the top well with *salt*, and leave them for *two days*.

> N.B.—We must turn the slices every morning and evening, and sprinkle a handful of salt over the layers each time we turn them.

4. We then drain the *slices* on a hair sieve for *one day*.

5. We put a *gallon of vinegar*, *two blades of mace*, *twenty-four cloves*, *twenty-four allspice berries*, and *twenty-four peppercorns* into a saucepan, with *three pieces of ginger an inch* long.

6. We put the saucepan on the fire and let it boil up.

7. We then turn the *vinegar and spices* out of the saucepan into a broad pan to cool.

> N.B.—They must on no account be allowed to cool in the saucepan.

8. We put the *cabbage* into a stone jar, and pour the *vinegar and spices* over it.

9. The *cabbage* must be quite covered with *vinegar*, and as it soaks it up more *vinegar* must be poured over it.

> N.B.—This quantity of *vinegar* is sufficient for a large *cabbage*; a smaller one will take less.

10. We tie the jar over with wash leather, brown paper, or a bladder. The *Pickle* is now ready for use.

'Lesson on Pickling Cabbage', from the text book of the National Training School for Cookery, South Kensington, London (c 1898)

14
Salting

One of the oldest methods of preservation known to man, salting is a highly effective way of preserving runner or French beans and white cabbage (sauerkraut). It is useful if there is a glut of either and a freezer is not available.

Beans

1 Choose young, fresh and tender beans. Top and tail. Remove strings from sides if necessary.

2 Leave French beans whole. Cut runner beans into thin, diagonal slices.

3 Pack well down into stone or glass jars, alternately with layers of salt sprinkled over the beans in liberal amounts. Begin and end with a thick layer of salt and keep pressing down the beans as you place each layer in the jar. Allow ½kg (1lb) kitchen salt (not table salt) to every 1½kg (3lb) beans.

4 Cover and leave in a cool, dark place for about 4 days. You will find that the beans have shrunk and the jar/jars should therefore be topped up with more beans and salt, once more finishing with a layer of salt.

5 As the salt draws moisture out of the beans, it will take on a liquid consistency and be-become a strong brine. Do not throw this away or pour out of the jar, as air pockets will form and the beans will, in consequence, deteriorate very quickly through the growth and development of mould and bacteria.

6 Finally insert a cork or cover with a piece of plastic material. Tie down very tightly.

7 Store stoneware jars on the shelf of a cupboard but do not leave on stone, brick or concrete surfaces as moisture will be drawn upwards.

8 The beans will easily keep 6 months. Before use, wash as many as are required in several changes of cold water.

9 Soak 2 hours *only* in warm water. Cook about ½ hour or until tender in boiling, unsalted water. Drain. Serve as fresh beans.

Sauerkraut

Sauerkraut has been a way of life in Central and parts of Northern Europe for many hundreds of years.

1 Allow 15g (½oz) salt to every ½kg (1lb) white cabbage. Shred small heads of the cabbage finely and mix with the salt.

2 Pack tightly into a clean wooden tub or other suitable container such as a large crockpot with a wide neck.

3 Cover with a clean cloth. Then add a stopper which fits *inside* the tub or container. Press down with a heavy garden stone or brick.

4 Leave about 4 to 5 days, when the stopper should be under the surface of the liquid; the liquid in this case being brine made from the salt and water drawn out of the cabbage.

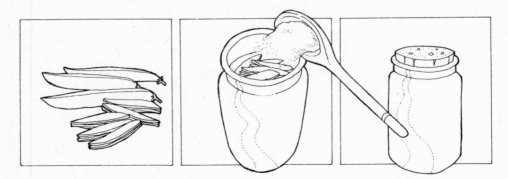

74

5 Leave about 2–3 weeks in a warm place – about 24°C or 75°F – while fermentation takes place. Remove scum from the surface every 3–4 days.

6 As fermentation decreases, you will probably need to add brine to bring the level over the lid again. Therefore use a solution made from 25g (1oz) salt to 1¼ litres (2pt) water.

7 After the 2–3 weeks, the sauerkraut is ready for use. Should you, however, wish to preserve it, drain off the brine into a large pan. Bring to the boil, and add cabbage.

8 Bring just up to simmering point. Pack straight away into heated preserving jars, adjust lids and process in boiling water for 25 minutes (see chapter on Bottling if you are unsure about the method). Remove jars, adjust seals and leave to cool.

Beans have been salted in much the same way for generations.

After deciding to leave home I gave instructions that the young French Beans and Scarlet Runners should be picked over, almost daily, so that none should grow coarse and old; and that the cook should lay them separately, as they were brought in, in large earthenware pans—a handful of Beans and then a handful of salt, and so on till the pan was full. This is an excellent method; and I have eaten them, preserved in this way, all through the winter. I believe this is done everywhere abroad, but never in England, where the waste, both in the kitchen and the garden, is, as we all acknowledge, a national vice. Of course the Beans in the salt must not be allowed to get touched by frost in the autumn. When wanted, they are taken out, well soaked (to prevent their being too salt), boiled in the ordinary way—cut up or whole, as we like them best—then drained, and warmed up in fresh butter, a squeeze of lemon and a little chopped Parsley on the top. They can also be cooked with a white cream sauce. I think these salted Beans have more flavour than the tinned ones, or than those that come from Madeira in the winter. Besides, the principle of utilising everything in a garden should never be lost sight of.

From Mrs C. W. Earle, *Pot-Pourri from a Surrey Garden* (c 1899)

15
Sauces

In the main, these are an extension of chutneys. For those who enjoy tasty sauces which resemble bought varieties of ketchup, they can be made simply enough.

Blend any cooked chutney (after first removing bag of spices) to a smooth purée in a blender goblet. Then thin out, if necessary, to a thickish, pouring consistency with boiled and cooled malt vinegar.

The sauces should be poured into bottles and tied down with Porosan Skin or corked. Store in the same way as chutney.

Plums, damsons and rhubarb make especially interesting sauces and recipes will be found under individual entries.

Mushroom Ketchup

Have the mushrooms gathered in the morning before the sun is on them. Break them in small pieces, put them in a large dish, and sprinkle a good deal of salt on them; let them lie for four days, turning them daily, then lay them on a sieve, or put them in a thin bag, and let them run all night until the liquor is all run from them. Take the mushrooms out of the bag, put them on in a little cold water, let them boil slowly for about half an hour, then drain, and add this second liquor to the first. Put the liquor in a stew-pan, with plenty of mixed spices, let it boil for five minutes, run it through a piece of muslin into a basin, and, when cold, bottle up, cork, seal, and keep it in a dry place.

From *Pears' Shilling Encyclopaedia* (c 1898)

Oyster Catsup

Take fine fresh Milton oysters, open them carefully, and wash them in their own liquor, to take any particle of shell that may remain, strain the liquor after. Pound the oysters in a mortar, add the liquor, and to every pint put a pint of sherry, boil it up and skim, then add two anchovies, pounded, an ounce of common salt, two drachms of pounded mace, and one of cayenne. Let it boil up, skim it, and rub it through a sieve. Bottle it when cold, and seal it. What remains in the sieve will do for oyster sauce.

From W. G. Lewis, *The Cook* (19th century)

PART II
A-Z of Fruits and Vegetables

Please read the appropriate section in Part I for each method of preserving suggested in the following list.

A

Apple and Apricot (Dried) Chutney

Follow recipe for Apple Chutney, but instead of apples, use ½kg (1lb) dried apricots (first soaked overnight) and 1kg (2lb) apples. About 75g (3oz) thinly sliced Brazil nuts may be stirred in at the end for a touch of novelty.

Apples, Baked and Frozen

Prepare cooking apples for baking according to your usual recipe. Pack centres with dried fruit, sugar, grated lemon or orange peel, syrup, honey, jam etc. Cook for half the length of time specified. Leave until cold. Pack into containers. Seal and label. Freeze up to 6 months. Thaw about 3 to 4 hours at kitchen temperature. Complete cooking in the oven before serving.

Apple and Bilberry Jam

For a yield of 2¼kg (5lb) use:
1kg (2lb) apples (weighed *after* peeling and coring), ½kg (1lb) bilberries, 150ml (¼pt) water and 1½kg (3lb) sugar.
For instructions, see Jam section.

Note : The bilberry – a blue-coloured berry – is also called the blaeberry (in Scotland) and whortleberry in the south.

Apple and Bilberry Jelly

Follow recipe for Apple Jelly but instead of apples only, use 1kg (2lb) cooking apples and 1kg (2lb) bilberries. Continue as directed in Jelly section, allowing 350g (12oz) sugar to every 575ml (1pt) juice.

Apple and Blackberry Butter

See sections on Fruit Cheeses and Butters.

Apple and Blackberry Cheese

See section on Fruit Cheeses. Use two-thirds apples and one-third blackberries.

Apple and Blackberry Jam

For a yield of 2¼kg (5lb) use:
350g (12oz) cooking apples (weighed *after* peeling and coring), 1kg (2lb) blackberries, 150ml (¼pt) water and 1½kg (3lb) sugar. For instructions, see Jam section.

Apple and Blackberry Jelly

Follow recipe for Apple Jelly but instead of apples, use 1kg (2lb) apples and 1kg (2lb) blackberries.

Apple and Blaeberry Jam

See Apple and Bilberry Jam.

Apples, Bottled (for dessert use)

Peel, core and slice apples. Place immediately in *boiling* water. Leave 2 to 3 minutes or until slices are pliable. Drain. Pack well down into jars. (Because of the flexibility of the slices, more will fit neatly into the jars and give you what is generally called a 'solid pack' of fruit). Treat exactly as Blackberries, Bottled, but adjust methods as follows:

Method 1
Raise temperature to 82°C (180°F) and maintain ¼ hour.

Method 2
Same temperature as Blackberries but maintain 20 minutes.

Method 3
Not recommended.

Method 4
Same temperature as Blackberries but process ½ to 2kg (1 to 4lb) for 50 to 60 minutes; 2¼ to 4½kg (5 to 10lb) for 65 to 80 minutes.

Method 5
Same process as for Blackberries but maintain pressure for 3 to 4 minutes.

For Methods 1 and 2, allow extra time for large size jars as given at the end of Blackberry entry.

Apples, Bottled (for pies, etc)

Peel, core and slice apples. To prevent excessive browning, drop apples into salt water made by dissolving 25g (1oz) salt in 2½ litres (4pt) water. Drain and rinse. Treat exactly as Blackberries, Bottled – see appropriate entry.

Apple Butter

See sections on Fruit Cheeses and Butters.

Apple Cheese

See section on Fruit Cheeses. Simmer apples in apple juice instead of water for a more pronounced apple flavour. For a spicy butter, add powdered cinnamon with the sugar, allowing 1 to 2 level teaspoons to every ½kg (1lb) apple pulp. Alternatively, add 6 cloves.

Apple Chutney

For a yield of 2¼kg (5lb) use:

1kg (2lb) onions, water, 2kg (4lb) apples (garden windfalls may be used but allow an extra ½kg (1lb) for wastage), 3 to 4 garlic cloves, 1¼ litres (2pt) malt vinegar, 225g (8oz) *each* chopped dates and sultanas, ¾kg (1½lb) soft brown sugar (dark variety), 2 level teaspoons *each* ground cinnamon and ginger, 1 level teaspoon mixed spice, ¼ to ½ level teaspoon cayenne pepper (optional), 3 to 4 level teaspoons salt, 1 muslin bag containing 1 level teaspoon mixed pickling spice, 1 medium-sized bay leaf and 4 cloves.

Chop onions fairly finely and put into large pan. Add just enough water to cover. Put on lid. Simmer ¼ hour. Peel and core apples. Chop or coarsely mince with peeled garlic. Add to pan with half the vinegar and all remaining ingredients. Bring to boil, stirring. Lower heat. Cover. Simmer gently ¾ hour. Stir occasionally. Add rest of vinegar. Bring to boil, stirring. Lower heat. Cook, uncovered, for about 2 hours or until chutney is deep tan in colour and with a thick, jam-like consistency. Remove bag of spices. Pot and cover as directed in Chutney section.

Apple and Clove Jam

Wash and dry 1½kg (3lb) sour apples. Roughly cut up without peeling or coring. Put into pan. Add 575ml (1pt) water, 8 cloves and 2 level teaspoons citric acid (available from pharmacies). Cook, covered, until apples are very pulpy.

Continue to cook, uncovered, until mixture has reduced by about one-third. Rub the fruit through a fine mesh sieve and discard fibrous pieces of fruit as well as the cloves. Measure pulp and allow 350g (12oz) granulated sugar to every ½kg (1lb) pulp. Put both together in clean pan. Stir over low heat till sugar dissolves. Boil rapidly until setting point is reached. Pot and cover as directed in Jam section.

Apple and Cranberry Butter

See sections on Fruit Cheeses and Fruit Butters.

Apple and Cranberry Cheese

See section on Fruit Cheeses. Use equal amounts of apples and cranberries.

Apple and Cranberry Jam

See Cranberry Jam. Use ¾kg (1½lb) sour apples, weighed after peeling and coring, and ½kg (1lb) fresh cranberries. Keep amount of sugar and water the same. Simmer apples and cranberries in the water until soft and pulpy. Add sugar. Continue as directed in Jam section.

Apple and Cranberry Jelly

See sections on Jellies and Jams. Follow recipe for Apple Jelly but instead of apples only, use 1kg (2lb) cooking apples and 1kg (2lb) cranberries.

Apple and Damson Jam

See Damson Jam. Use half amount of apples and half of damsons.

Apples, Dried

Choose Bramley Seedlings or any variety of good eating apples. Windfalls are perfectly acceptable as well.

Peel and core fruit, at the same time removing blemishes. Cut into 6mm (¼in) slices and drop into a salt water solution made by dissolving 25g (1oz) salt in every 2½ litres (4pt) water. Leave 5 minutes, remove from salt water and tip into colander. Shake to remove as much surplus water as possible.

Continue as described in section on drying. Allow about 4 to 6 hours drying time if the process is continuous, or a period of 2 to 3 days if the heat is intermittent. The apple rings are ready when they look like chamois leather.

Note: If preferred, the rings may be threaded on to sticks and laid in parallel lines on trays. This takes up less space than arranging them flat.

Apple and Elderberry Chutney

Follow recipe for Apple Chutney but use 1kg (2lb) apples and 1kg (2lb) ripe elderberries.

Apple and Fig Jam

See Fig and Apple Jam.

Apple and Ginger Jam

For a yield of around 3kg (6½lb):
Peel and core 2kg (4lb) cooking apples and slice directly into pan. Add peel and cores tied in a piece of cloth or put into muslin bag. Pour in just over ¾ litre (1½pt) water. Simmer, uncovered, over low heat until fruit is very soft and pulpy. Remove bag of peel etc. Beat apples to a light purée or blend until smooth in blender goblet.

Return mixture to pan with 1½kg (3lb) sugar, 225g (8oz) finely chopped preserved ginger, 4 tablespoons ginger syrup, 1 level teaspoon powdered ginger and the grated peel and juice of 3 medium lemons. Stir over low heat until sugar dissolves. Boil until setting point is reached. Pot and cover as directed in Jam section.

Apple Jelly

Cut 2kg (4lb) cooking apples into thick slices without peeling or coring. Simmer with 1¼ litres (2pt) water for about 1 hour. Continue as directed in Jelly section, allowing ½kg (1lb) sugar to every 575ml (1pt) juice.

Apple Lemon Jelly

Follow recipe for Apple Jelly, but add strips of 2 medium-sized lemons when simmering the fruit.

Apple and Marrow Chutney

Follow recipe for Apple Chutney, but use 1kg (2lb) apples and 1kg (2lb) de-rinded, de-seeded and cubed marrow.

Apples, Mincemeat

See section on Mincemeat. Use dessert apples.

Apple and Mulberry Jelly

Follow recipe for Apple Jelly, but instead of apples only, use 1kg (2lb) cooking apples and 1kg (2lb) mulberries.

Apple and Orange Jam

Follow recipe for Apple and Clove Jam, but omit cloves. Instead add 2 level teaspoons powdered cinnamon and the finely grated peel of 2 medium oranges with the sugar.

Apple and Plum Jam

For a yield of 2¼kg (5lb) use:
¾kg (1½lb) stoned plums, ¾kg (1½lb) sour apples (weighed *after* peeling and coring), 275ml (½pt) water and 1½kg (3lb) sugar. For instructions, see Jam section.

Apple and Plum Chutney

Follow recipe for Apple Chutney, but use 1kg (2lb) apples and 1kg (2lb) plums.

Apple and Plum Sauce

Make up Plum and Apple Chutney then continue as directed for Sauces.

Apple, Pulped and Frozen

See section on Freezing with particular reference to Fruit Purées. For apples, follow Method 2. Store up to one year.

Apple and Rhubarb Butter

See sections on Fruit Cheeses and Butters.

Apple and Rhubarb Cheese

See section on Fruit Cheeses. Use equal amounts of apples and prepared rhubarb.

Apple and Rhubarb Chutney

Follow recipe for Apple Chutney, but instead of apples use 1kg (2lb) apples and 1kg (2lb) rhubarb (trimmed weight).

Apple and Rhubarb Sauce

Make up Apple and Rhubarb Chutney then continue as directed for Sauces.

Apple and Rowan Berry Jelly

Follow recipe for Apple Jelly, but instead of apples only, use 1kg (2lb) cooking apples and 1 kg (2lb) rowan berries.

Note: Vivid red rowans are berries from the mountain ash tree and are popular in Scotland. They are about the size of peas.

Apples, Sliced and Frozen

Choose a trusted cooking variety such as Bramleys. Peel, core and slice. Blanch 1½ to 3 minutes or until apple slices are pliable. (See Blanching of Vegetables p 29.) Freeze in syrup as described under Method 2 in Freezing section. Store up to one year.

Apple and Sloe Jelly

Follow recipe for Apple Jelly, but instead of apples only, use 1kg (2lb) cooking apples and 1kg (2lb) sloes. Reduce water to 575ml

(1pt). Continue as directed in Jelly section, allowing ½kg (1lb) sugar to every 575ml (1pt) juice.

Note: Sloes are dark, purplish-black berries with an acrid taste. They grow on blackthorn bushes and are used to flavour sloe gin.

Apple Spice Jelly

Follow recipe for Apple Jelly, but add 2 to 3 level teaspoons ground ginger and/or cinnamon when simmering the fruit. About 6 to 8 cloves may be used in preference to the other spices.

Apples, Stewed and Frozen

Treat *exactly* as Fruit, Stewed and Frozen – see appropriate entry.

Apples, Sweet-Sour

Follow recipe for Crab Apples, Sweet-Sour. Halve *unpeeled* apples and remove cores before simmering in the sweetened vinegar. Pricking the skin is unnecessary.

Apple and Whortleberry Jam

See Apple and Bilberry Jam.

Apple and Whortleberry Jelly

This is identical to Apple and Bilberry Jelly – see appropriate entry.

Apricots in Alcohol

See section on Fruits in Alcohol with special reference to the Rum Pot and Apricots in Brandy.

Apricots, Bottled

Wash and dry apricots. Cut in half and remove stones. Pack into jars, adding a few kernels removed from cracked stones. Treat *exactly* as Blackberries, Bottled, but adjust methods as follows:

Method 1
Raise temperature to 82°C (180°F) and maintain ¼ hour.

Method 2
Same temperature as blackberries but maintain 20 minutes.

Method 3
Not recommended.

Method 4
Same temperature as blackberries but process ½ to 2kg (1 to 4lb) for 50 to 60 minutes; 2¼ to 4½kg (5 to 10lb) for 65 to 80 minutes.

Method 5
Same process as blackberries but maintain pressure for 3 to 4 minutes.

For Methods 1 and 2, allow extra time for large-size jars as given at the end of blackberry entry.

Apricots in Brandy

See section on Fruits in Alcohol.

Apricots, Dried

See Apples, Dried. Also read section on Drying.

Wash and dry apricots. Cut in half with a stainless knife. Remove stones. Arrange on trays, cut sides uppermost. Some browning

will occur but this is expected and perfectly acceptable.

Allow about 5 to 7 hours' drying time if the process is continuous, or for a period of 3 to 4 days if the heat is intermittent. The apricots are ready when they look leathery and no juice leaks out when fruit is squeezed.

Apricots (Dried) and Apple Chutney

Follow recipe for Apple Chutney, but instead of apples, use ½kg (1lb) dried apricots (first soaked overnight) and 1kg (2lb) apples. About 75g (3oz) thinly sliced Brazil nuts may be stirred in at the end for a touch of novelty.

Apricots (Dried) and Cognac Jam

Follow recipe for Dried Apricot Jam, adding 3 tablespoons Cognac with the almonds.

Apricot (Dried) Jam

For a yield of 2¼kg (5lb):
Well-wash ½kg (1lb) dried apricots. Put into large pan. Add 1¾ litres (3pt) water. Leave overnight to soak. Add juice of 2 medium lemons. Bring slowly to boil. Cover. Lower heat. Simmer till fruit is *very soft*. Add 1½kg (3lb) sugar and stir until dissolved. Add 50 to 75g (2 to 3oz) blanched almonds, first cut into slivers. Boil briskly until setting point is reached. Pot and cover as described in Jam section.

Apricot (Dried) and Mandarin Jam

Follow recipe for Dried Apricot Jam, adding the finely grated peel of 2 or 3 mandarins with the almonds.

Apricot (Fresh) Jam

For a yield of 2¼kg (5lb) use:
1½kg (3lb) halved and stoned apricots, 275ml (½pt) water, juice of 1 large lemon and 1½kg (3lb) sugar. For instructions, see Jam section.

Apricots, Frozen

Wash and gently dry ripe apricots. Halve and remove stones. Sprinkle cut surfaces with lemon juice. Freeze in syrup as described under Method 2. For making jam, toss whole fruit in sugar before freezing. Pack into containers. Seal and label. Freeze whole apricots for 6 months; halved and stoned apricots for one year.

Apricot and Peach Chutney

Follow recipe for Apple Chutney, but instead of apples, use 1kg (2lb) skinned fresh peaches and 1kg (2lb) skinned fresh apricots. Cut both into chunks.

Note: To skin fruit, cover with boiling water and leave 1 minute. Drain. Cover with cold water. Leave 1 minute. Slide off skins.

Apricot and Peach Sauce

Make up Apricot and Peach Chutney then continue as directed for Sauces.

Apricots, Pulped and Frozen

See section on Freezing with particular reference to Fruit Purées. Follow either Methods 1 or 2. Skin apricots first by covering with boiling water, leaving for 1 minute, draining and then covering with cold water. When cool enough to handle, peel fruit with a stainless knife. Store up to one year.

Apricots, Stewed and Frozen

See section on Freezing. Treat *exactly* as Fruit, Stewed and Frozen – see appropriate entry.

Apricots, Whole Bottled

Wash apricots and wipe dry. Treat *exactly* as Cherries, Red and Black - see appropriate entry.

It is important to note that apricots should *not* be bottled by Method 3 (slow oven).

Artichokes, Globe and Frozen

Choose young and tender artichokes. Strip off outer leaves and cut off stems. Also cut off tips of leaves at top of each. Blanch three at a time, allowing 6 minutes for small artichokes and 8 minutes for large ones. Freeze separately in polythene bags. Store up to one year.

Note: A tablespoon of lemon juice added to the blanching water helps to keep the vegetables from turning dark.

Asparagus, Frozen

Scrape asparagus stems but take care not to damage tips. Trim to fit container, which should be of rigid plastic. Blanch thick stems for 4 minutes; thin stems for 2 minutes. Pack tips to stalks. Freeze up to one year.

Aubergines, Frozen

Choose medium-sized and plump aubergines. Wash well and dry and remove stems and surrounding leaves. Either halve lengthwise or peel and cut into slices or dice. Blanch halves 5 minutes; slices or dice, 4 minutes. Pack into containers and store up to one year.

B

Banana Chutney (West African)

For a yield of 1½kg (3lb):

Chop up 12 bananas, ½kg (1lb) green tomatoes and 225g (8oz) onions. Put all ingredients into pan with 225g (8oz) seedless raisins, 2 de-seeded green or red peppers (cut into thin strips), 225g (8oz) brown sugar, 275ml (½pt) vinegar and 3 to 4 level teaspoons salt. Bring to boil, stirring. Simmer gently, uncovered, until the consistency of jam – about 1½ to 2 hours. Stir from time to time. Keeps indefinitely.

Banana and Cranberry Chutney

Follow recipe for Apple Chutney, but instead of apples, use 1½kg (3lb) cranberries and ½kg (1lb) bananas (weighed after peeling).

Banana and Rhubarb Chutney

Follow recipe for Apple Chutney, but instead of apples, use 1kg (2lb) rhubarb (trimmed weight) and 1kg (2lb) bananas (peeled weight). If liked, substitute dried figs for dates.

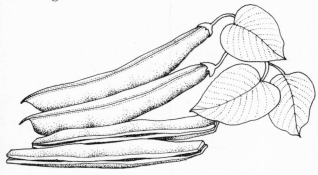

Beans, Broad and Frozen

Remove beans from pods. Blanch 3 minutes. Freeze in polythene bags or containers. For beans which stay separate during storage, follow 'Free Flow' method of freezing described on page 29. Store up to one year.

Note: Do not freeze large, over-mature beans which will be very tough.

Beans (Dwarf) Dried

See section on Drying.

Beans (French)

See section on Salting.

Beans (French) Frozen

Top and tail beans and remove side strings if necessary. If very large, cut into pieces measuring 2½cm (1in). Blanch 3 minutes if whole; 2 minutes if cut. Freeze in polythene bags or containers. For beans which stay separate, follow 'Free Flow' method of freezing described on page 29. Store up to one year.

Beans (Runner) Dried

See section on Drying.

Beans (Runner) Frozen

Top and tail beans and remove side strings. Blanch 3 minutes. Cut into thin, diagonal slices. Freeze in polythene bags or containers. For beans which stay separate, follow 'Free Flow' method of freezing described on page 29. Store up to one year.

Beans (Runner) Salted

See section on Salting.

Beetroot, Cooked and Frozen

Choose young, cooked beets and remove skins. Slice or dice flesh. Pack into plastic containers and freeze up to 6 months. *Do not* blanch.

Beetroot, Pickled

Peel required amount of cooked beetroots. Slice or dice. Pack into jars, lightly sprinkling salt between layers. Fill with cold spiced vinegar. Cover. Leave about 1 to 2 weeks before eating.

Bilberry and Apple Jelly

Follow recipe for Apple Jelly, but instead of

apples only, use 1kg (2lb) cooking apples and 1kg (2lb) bilberries. Continue as directed in Jelly section, allowing 350g (12oz) sugar to every 575ml (1pt) juice.

Bilberries, Bottled

Choose fruit in prime condition. Treat *exactly* as Blackberries, Bottled – see entry.

Bilberries, Frozen

See section on Freezing. Follow methods 2 or 3. Store up to one year.

Bilberry Jam

For a yield of 2½kg (5½lb) use:
1½kg (3lb) bilberries, 150ml (¼pt) water, juice of 2 large lemons, 1 × 225ml bottle (8 fl oz) commercial pectin and 1½kg (3lb) sugar. For instructions, see Jam section.

Bilberry and Apple Jam

See Apple and Bilberry Jam.

Bilberries, Stewed and Frozen

Treat *exactly* as Fruit, Stewed and Frozen – see appropriate entry.

Bilberry Syrup

See section on Fruit Syrups
Make by Methods 1 or 2, adding *no* water. Allow 350g (12oz) sugar to every 575ml (1pt) strained fruit juice.

Bitter Orange Marmalade

Made the same way as Seville Orange Marmalade – see appropriate entry.

Blackberry and Apple Butter

See sections on Fruit Cheeses and Fruit Butters.

Blackberry and Apple Cheese

See section on Fruit Cheeses. Use two-thirds apples and one-third blackberries.

Blackberry and Apple Jam

See Apple and Blackberry Jam.

Blackberry and Apple Jelly

Follow recipe for Apple Jelly but instead of apples, use 1kg (2lb) apples and 1kg (2lb) blackberries.

Blackberries, Bottled

Select the method, from 1 to 5, that is the most practical and/or convenient for your own needs. Make sure fruit is in prime condition. Pack into jars.

Method 1
Fill jars with cold water or syrup. Fit on lids etc. Immerse in cold water. Raise temperature to 74°C (165°F) in 1½ hours. Maintain 10 minutes.

Method 2

Fill fruit-packed jars with hot water or syrup. Fit on lids etc. Immerse jars in luke-warm water (blood heat). Bring water to simmering point (88°C or 190°F) in ½ hour. Maintain jars at simmering temperature for 2 minutes.

Method 3

Stand fruit-packed jars on trays. Put into oven preheated for ¼ hour to 120°C (250°F), Gas ½. Process ½ to 2kg (1 to 4lb) for 45 to 55 minutes; 2¼ to 4½kg (5 to 10lb) for 60 to 75 minutes. Fill *after* processing with boiling water or syrup. Attach rings, lids etc.

Method 4

Stand fruit-packed jars on trays. Fill with boiling water or syrup. Add rubber rings and lids but *do not* attach screw bands or clips. Put into oven preheated for ¼ hour to 150°C (300°F), Gas 2. Process ½ to 2kg (1 to 4lb) for 30 to 40 minutes; 2¼ to 4½kg (5 to 10lb) for 45 to 60 minutes.

Method 5

Fill jars with fruit and boiling water or syrup. Fit on rubber bands, lids, screw bands or clips. Loosen screw bands by ¼ turn.

Stand 1 or 2 jars in pressure cooker containing 2½cm (1in) boiling water. Cover. Heat till steam comes out of vent. Add 2½kg (5lb) weight. Bring up to pressure over period of 5 to 10 minutes. Maintain pressure for 1 minute. Continue as directed on page 14 in Method 5.

For large jars bottled by Methods 1 and 2, allow extra time as follows: 1½ and 2kg (3 and 4lb), 5 minutes; 2¼ and 2¾kg (5 and 6lb) 10 minutes; 3¼ and 3¾kg (7 and 8lb), 15 minutes.

Blackberry and Elderberry Jam

See Elderberry and Blackberry Jam.

Blackberry and Elderberry Jelly

See sections on Jellies and Jams. Follow recipe for Apple Jelly but instead of apples, use 1kg (2lb) elderberries and 1kg (2lb) blackberries. Simmer fruits with the juice of 2 lemons and only 275ml (½pt) water.

Blackberries, Frozen

See section on Freezing. Follow either Methods 1, 2 or 3, depending on personal requirements. Store up to one year.

Blackberry Jam

For a yield of 2¼kg (5lb), use:
1½kg (3lb) just-ripe blackberries, 5 table-spoons water, 2 tablespoons lemon juice, 1½kg (3lb) sugar. For instructions, see Jam section.

Blackberry (Frozen) Jam

Read Freezer Jams in Jam section on page 54. For a yield of about 1¾kg (3½lb) use:
550g (1¼lb) blackberries, 3 tablespoons lemon juice, 1¼kg (2½lb) sugar, ½ bottle (4 fl oz or 125ml) liquid pectin.

Blackberry Jelly

This is identical to Bramble Jelly – see appropriate entry.

Blackberry and Mulberry Jam

See Blackberry Jam. Use half blackberries and half mulberries. Keep the amounts of water, lemon juice and sugar the same.

Blackberry and Mulberry Syrup

See section on Fruit Syrups. Make by Methods 1 or 2, adding *no* water. Allow 350g (12oz) sugar to every 575ml (1pt) strained fruit juice.

Blackberries, Pickled

Dissolve ½kg (1lb) granulated or preserving sugar in 275ml (½pt) spiced vinegar. Bring to the boil. Add 1kg (2lb) prepared fruit. Simmer gently just long enough to cook the fruit. Avoid overcooking or the fruit will disintegrate. Drain. Pack fruit into bottles. Boil sweetened vinegar until thick and syrupy. Pour over fruit. Cover while hot.

Blackberry and Plum Jam

See Plum Jam. Use 1kg (2lb) cooking plums and ½kg (1lb) blackberries. Keep amounts of water and sugar the same.

Blackberry and Redcurrant Jelly

See sections on Jellies and Jams. Follow recipe for Apple Jelly, but instead of apples, use ½kg (1lb) blackberries and 1½kg (3lb) redcurrants.

Blackberries, Stewed and Frozen

Treat exactly as Fruit, Stewed and Frozen – see appropriate entry.

Blackberry Syrup

See section on Fruit Syrups. Follow instructions, adding 275ml (½pt) water to every 3½kg (6lb) blackberries. Make by Methods 1 or 2, allowing 350g (12oz) sugar to every 575ml (1pt) strained fruit juice.

Blackcurrants in Alcohol

See section on Fruits in Alcohol.

Blackcurrants, Bottled

Stalk currants. Treat exactly as Blackberries, Bottled – see appropriate entry.

Blackcurrant Butter

See sections on Fruit Cheeses and Butters.

Blackcurrant Cheese

See section on Fruit Cheeses. Cook the blackcurrants long and slowly in water until *very* soft.

Blackcurrants, Frozen

See section on Freezing. Follow either Methods 1, 2 or 3, depending on personal requirements. Store up to one year.

Blackcurrant Jam

For a yield of 2¼kg (5lb) use: 1¼kg (2½lb) blackcurrants, ¾ litre (1½pt) water and 1½kg (3lb) sugar. For instructions, see Jam section.

Blackcurrant Jelly

Follow recipe for Apple Jelly, but instead of apples, use 2kg (4lb) blackcurrants.

Black and Redcurrants, Bottled

See section on Bottling. Stalk currants. Treat exactly as Blackberries, Bottled – see appropriate entry.

Blackcurrant and Redcurrant Jam

See Blackcurrant Jam. Use half black-currants and half redcurrants. Keep amounts of water and sugar the same.

Blackcurrants, Stewed and Frozen

See section on Freezing. Treat exactly as Fruit, Stewed and Frozen – see appropriate entry.

Blackcurrant Syrup

See section on Fruit Syrups. Follow instructions, adding 275ml (½pt) water to every ½kg (1lb) blackcurrants. Make by Methods 1 or 2, allowing 350g (12oz) sugar to every 575ml (1pt) strained fruit juice.

Blaeberry and Apple Jam

See Apple and Bilberry Jam.

Blaeberries, Bottled

See section on Bottling. Choose fruit in prime condition. Treat exactly as Black-berries, Bottled – see appropriate entry.

Blaeberries, Frozen

See section on Freezing. Follow Methods 2 or 3. Store up to one year.

Blaeberries, Stewed and Frozen

See section on Freezing. Treat exactly as Fruit, Stewed and Frozen – see appropriate entry.

Bramble Jelly

Follow recipe for Apple Jelly, but instead of

apples, use 2kg (4lb) blackberries. Simmer the fruit with the juice of 2 large lemons and only 275ml (½pt) water.

Note: If preferred, use 1 level teaspoon citric or tartaric acid instead of lemon juice.

Broccoli, Frozen

If broccoli is the same size as cauliflower, divide up into florets. Blanch 3 to 4 minutes. Pack into rigid containers. Store up to one year.

If using young heads (sprouting Broccoli for example), trim stems to fit container and pack heads to stalks in the same way as asparagus.

Brussels Sprouts, Frozen

Choose small, tight sprouts. Remove outer leaves and make a cut in the stalk end of each. Blanch 3 minutes. Freeze in polythene bags or containers. Store up to one year.

For sprouts which stay separate during storage, follow 'Free Flow' method of freezing described on page 29.

C

Cabbage, Frozen

Choose young, firm cabbage (white or green), discard any damaged outer leaves and cut into strips of about 6mm (¼in).

Blanch 1 or 2 minutes, depending on coarseness of cabbage. Freeze in polythene bags or containers. Store up to six months.

Cabbage (White) Salted

See section on Salting.

Calabrese, Frozen

See Broccoli, Frozen.

Calvados

See footnote in Fruits in Alcohol section.

Carrots, Spring or New, Frozen

Scrape carrots and cut off tops. Wash well. Blanch 6 minutes. Freeze in polythene bags or containers. Store up to one year.

Note: Whole carrots are best frozen in serving sized amounts.

Carrots, Winter or Old, Frozen

Choose medium-sized, crisp carrots. Peel and dice. Blanch 4 to 5 minutes. Freeze in polythene bags or containers. Store up to one year. For carrot dice which stay separate during storage, follow 'Free Flow' method of freezing described on page 29.

Note: Carrot dice and peas may be frozen together.

Cauliflower, Frozen

Choose cauliflowers in prime condition. Break into florets. Blanch 3 minutes. Freeze in polythene bags or containers. Store up to one year.

For cauliflower florets which stay separate during storage, follow 'Free Flow' method of freezing described on page 29.

Cauliflower, Pickled

Divide cauliflower into small florets and put into bowl. Cover completely with brine. Keep vegetable immersed by covering with plate weighed down with heavy garden stone. Leave 24 hours. Drain. Rinse. Drain thoroughly again. Pack into jars. Fill with cold spiced vinegar. Cover. Leave for about six to eight weeks before eating.

Celery, Frozen

Choose young, crisp stalks and pull off strings. Cut into 2½cm (1in) lengths. Blanch 2 minutes. Freeze in polythene bags or containers. Store up to six months. Use in cooked dishes *only*.

Cherries in Alcohol

See section on Fruits in Alcohol, and the Rum Pot in particular.

Cherries in Brandy

See section on Fruits in Alcohol.

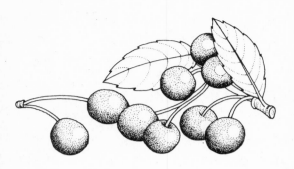

Cherries, Frozen

Choose dark red or black cherries. Halve and remove stones, collecting juice. Follow either Method 2 or 3, adding juice to syrup (Method 2) or tossing it with fruit and sugar (Method 3). Store up to one year.

Cherry and Gooseberry Jam

See Gooseberry Jam. Use 1kg (2lb) gooseberries and ½kg (1lb) stoned dessert cherries, weighed *after* stoning. Keep amounts of water and sugar the same.

Cherry Jam

For a yield of about 2½kg (5½lb) use:
2kg (4lb) stoned dessert cherries, juice of 3 large lemons, 1½kg (3lb) sugar and 2 bottles of commercial pectin (each 225ml or 8 fl oz). For instructions, see Jam section.

Note: The addition of acid (lemon juice) and pectin is necessary because dessert cherries are low in both.

Cherries (Light-coloured) Bottled

Stalk cherries but leave whole. Treat exactly as Cherries, Red and Black – see appropriate entry.

It is important to note that light-coloured cherries should *not* be bottled by Method 3 (slow oven).

Cherries, Morello in Alcohol

See section on Fruits in Alcohol, with special reference to the Rum Pot and Cherries in Brandy.

Cherries, Red and Black, Bottled

Stalk cherries but leave whole. Pack tightly into jars.

Method 1
Fill jars with cold water or syrup. Fit on lids, etc. Immerse in cold water. Raise temperature to 82°C (180°F) in 1½ hours. Maintain ¼ hour.

Method 2
Fill fruit-packed jars with hot water or syrup. Fit on lids, etc. Immerse jars in lukewarm water (blood heat). Bring water to simmering point (88°C or 190°F) in ½ hour. Maintain jars at simmering temperature for 10 minutes.

Method 3
Stand fruit-packed jars on trays. Put into oven preheated for ¼ hour to 120°C (250°F), Gas ½. Process ½ to 2kg (1 to 4lb) for 55 to 70 minutes; 2¼ to 4½kg (5 to 10lb) for 75 to 90 minutes. Fill *after* processing with boiling water or syrup. Attach rings, lids etc.

Method 4
Stand fruit-packed jars on trays. Fill with *boiling* water or syrup. Add rubber rings and lids but *do not* attach screwbands or clips. Put into oven preheated for ¼ hour to 150°C (300°F), Gas 2. Process ½ to 2kg (1 to 4lb)

for 30 to 40 minutes; $2\frac{1}{4}$ to $4\frac{1}{2}$kg (5 to 10lb) for 45 to 60 minutes.

Method 5
Fill jars with fruit and boiling water or syrup. Fit on rubber bands, lids, screw bands or clips. Loosen screw bands by $\frac{1}{4}$ turn. Stand 1 or 2 jars in pressure cooker containing $2\frac{1}{2}$cm (1in) boiling water. Cover. Heat till steam comes out of vent. Add $2\frac{1}{2}$kg (5lb) weight. Bring up to pressure over period of 5 to 10 minutes. Maintain pressure for 1 minute. Continue as directed on page 14 in Method 5.

For large jars bottled by Methods 1 and 2, allow extra time as follows: $1\frac{1}{2}$ and 2kg (3 and 4lb), 5 minutes; $2\frac{1}{4}$ and $2\frac{3}{4}$kg (5 and 6lb) 10 minutes; $3\frac{1}{4}$ and $3\frac{3}{4}$kg (7 and 8lb), 15 minutes.

Cherries, Stewed and Frozen

Treat exactly as Fruit, Stewed and Frozen – see appropriate entry.

Chinese Gooseberries, Bottled

Identical to Kiwi Fruit, Bottled – see appropirate entry.

Chinese Gooseberries, Frozen

See Kiwi Fruit, Frozen.

Chips, Frozen

See Potato Chips, Frozen.

Citrus Chutney

Follow recipe for Apple Chutney, but instead of apples, use 1kg (2lb) oranges, 225g (8oz) grapefruit, 225g (8oz) lemons and $\frac{1}{2}$kg (1lb) cooking pears. Wash and dry citrus fruits. *Do not peel*. Cut into cubes, discarding pips. Peel and dice pears.

Clementine and Lime Marmalade

For a yield of $2\frac{1}{4}$kg (5lb) use:
$\frac{1}{2}$kg (1lb) limes, 225g (8oz) clementines, $1\frac{3}{4}$ litres (3pt) water and $1\frac{1}{2}$kg (3lb) sugar. Choose the most convenient method, for personal requirements, from Nos 1 to 4 in Marmalade section, pp 63–65.

Clementine and Plum Jam

See Plum Jam. For an unusual and fragrant flavour, allow the finely grated peel of 2 clementines to every $1\frac{1}{2}$kg (3lb) fruit and add with the sugar.

Clove and Apple Jam

See Apple and Clove Jam.

Cognac and Apricot (Dried) Jam

See Apricot (Dried) and Cognac Jam.

Corn on the Cob, Frozen

Choose young cobs with creamy pearl-coloured kernels. Remove husks and silks. Blanch cobs 4 to 6 minutes. Pack separately or in twos. Store up to one year.

Courgettes, Frozen

Choose courgettes no longer than 15cm (6in). Leave whole or cut into thick slices. Blanch whole courgettes for 2 minutes; slices for 1 minute. Freeze in polythene bags or containers. Store up to six months.

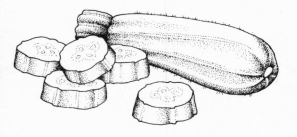

Crab Apple Butter

See sections on Fruit Cheeses and Butters.

Crab Apple Cheese

See section on Fruit Cheeses.
Simmer crab apples in water or half water and half orange juice. For a spicy butter, add powdered cinnamon with the sugar, allowing 1 to 2 level teaspoons to every ½kg (1lb) apple pulp.

Crab Apple Jelly

Follow recipe for Apple Jelly, substituting crab apples for cooking apples.

Crab Apple and Plum Butter

See sections on Fruit Cheeses and Butters.

Crab Apple and Plum Cheese

See section on Fruit Cheeses. Use equal amounts of stoned plums and cut-up crab apples.

Crab Apple Spice Jelly

Follow recipe for Apple Jelly, substituting crab apples for cooking apples. Add 2 to 3 level teaspoons ground ginger and/or cinnamon when simmering the fruit. About 6 to

8 cloves may be used in preference to the other spices.

Crab Apples, Sweet-Sour

Wash and dry 1kg (2lb) crab apples. Prick them lightly all over to prevent fruit shrivelling. Pour 575ml (1pt) spiced vinegar into pan. Add 1kg (2lb) granulated or preserving sugar. Dissolve over low heat. Add fruit. Simmer gently, covered, until tender. Do not overcook or fruit will break up. Carefully transfer crab apples to jars. Boil syrup fairly briskly until it is reduced to about 275ml (½pt). Pour into jars. Cover. Leave for about six weeks before eating.

Cranberries, Bottled

Discard any shrivelled or mildewed berries. Treat exactly as Blackberries, Bottled – see appropriate entry.

Cranberries, Frozen

Freeze as described under Method 1. Cook berries from frozen state with sugar and water before eating. Store up to six months.

Cranberries, Stewed and Frozen

Treat exactly as Fruit, Stewed and Frozen – see appropriate entry.

Cranberry and Apple Butter

See sections on Fruit Cheeses and Fruit Butters.

Cranberry and Apple Cheese

See section on Fruit Cheeses. Use equal amounts of apples and cranberries.

Cranberry and Apple Jam

See Cranberry Jam. Use ½kg (1lb) fresh cranberries and ¾kg (1½lb) sour apples, weighed *after* peeling and coring. Keep amount of sugar and water the same. Simmer apples and cranberries in the water until soft and pulpy. Add sugar. Continue as described in Jam section.

Cranberry and Apple Jelly

Follow recipe for Apple Jelly, but instead of apples only, use 1kg (2lb) cooking apples and 1kg (2lb) cranberries.

Cranberry and Banana Chutney

Follow recipe for Apple Chutney, but instead of apples, use 1½kg (3lb) cranberries and ½kg (1lb) bananas (weighed after peeling).

Cranberry Jam

For a yield of 2¼kg (5lb):
Put 1¼kg (2½lb) granulated sugar in pan. Add 575ml (1pt) water. Heat slowly until sugar dissolves. Bring to a brisk boil. Add 1kg (2lb) fresh cranberries. Cook a little more slowly until setting point is reached – about 20 minutes. Pot and cover as described in Jam section.

Cranberry and Orange Jam

See Cranberry Jam. Add finely grated peel of 1 large orange with the cranberries.

Cucumber, Pickled

Wash and dry required number of cucumbers. Leave unpeeled. Cut into thickish slices (about 2½cm or 1in). Soak 24 hours in brine. Drain and pack into jars. Fill with cold spiced vinegar. Cover. Leave about seven to eight days before eating.

Note: As cucumbers are inclined to soften quickly, it is advisable to use up the pickles within two weeks. Refrigerator storage helps to keep the cucumbers crisp.

Curd, Lemon

See section on Fruit Curds.

Curly Kale, Frozen

Pull leaves off stalks. Soak in cold salted water to remove grit. Shake dry. Blanch leaves 1 minute. Freeze in polythene bags or containers. Store up to six months.

Currants (Dried)

See section on Mincemeat.

Currants, Red, White and Black, Bottled

Stalk mixture of currants. Treat exactly as Blackberries, Bottled – see appropriate entry.

D

Damson and Apple Jam

See Damson Jam. Use half damsons and half cooking apples.

Damsons, Bottled

Stalk damsons then wash and dry. Treat exactly as Cherries, Red and Black – see appropriate entry.

Damson Butter

See sections on Fruit Cheeses and Butters.

Damson Cheese

See section on Fruit Cheeses. For an intesting and refreshing flavour, add 1 level teaspoon finely grated lemon peel with the sugar.

Damson Chutney

Follow recipe for Apple Chutney, but instead of apples, use 2kg (4lb) damsons. In order to remove stones easily, slit each damson and cook first in water with onions, *before* adding balance of ingredients. As the damsons tenderise, the stones will emerge and these should be carefully removed with a perforated draining spoon.

Damsons, Frozen

Wash and dry but leave whole. Freeze in syrup as described under Method 2. Store up to six months.

Damson Jam

For a yield of 2¼kg (5lb) use:
1¼kg (2½lb) damsons, 575ml (1pt) water and 1½kg (3lb) sugar. For instructions, see Jam section.

Note: Slit each damson so that stones come out more easily. Skim the stones off as they rise to the top during boiling.

Damson Jelly

Follow recipe for Apple Jelly, but instead of apples, use 2kg (4lb) damsons.

Damsons, Pickled

Simmer 2kg (4lb) stalked damsons in just over ¾ litre (1½pt) spiced vinegar until just tender. Pack fruit into jars. Fill with hot vinegar plus, if liked, a few juniper berries. Cover. Leave for three to four months before eating.

Damsons, Pulped and Frozen

See section on Freezing with particular reference to Fruit Purées. Follow Method 2, removing all stones. If liked, the fruit may be cooked with a little spice to taste. Store up to one year.

Damson Sauce

Make up Damson Chutney then continue as directed for Sauces.

Damsons, Stewed and Frozen

Treat exactly as Fruit, Stewed and Frozen – see appropriate entry.

Damsons, Sweet-Sour

Follow recipe for Pears, Sweet-Sour. To prepare damsons, remove stalks then wash and dry the fruit.

Dates

See section on Mincemeat. Use cooking dates that are stoned, compressed and sold in blocks.

Dried Produce

See under individual entries.

Duchesse Potatoes, Frozen

See Potatoes, Duchesse and Frozen.

E

Egg Plants, Frozen

See Aubergines, Frozen.

Elderberry and Apple Chutney

Follow recipe for Apple Chutney but use 1kg (2lb) apples and 1kg (2lb) ripe elderberries.

Elderberry and Blackberry Jam

For a yield of about 2¼kg (5lb) use: 1kg (2lb) elderberries, 1kg (2lb) blackberries, 5 tablespoons water and 1½kg (3lb) sugar. For instructions, see Jam section.

Elderberry and Blackberry Jelly

See sections on Jellies and Jams. Follow recipe for Apple Jelly but instead of apples, use 1kg (2lb) elderberries and 1kg (2lb) blackberries. Simmer fruit with the juice of 2 lemons and only 275ml (½pt) water.

Elderberries, Bottled

Choose fruit in prime condition and remove berries from stalks. Treat exactly as Blackberries, Bottled – see appropriate entry.

Elderberries, Frozen

Choose fruit in prime condition and remove from stalks. Blanch ½ minute (see blanching of vegetables, p 29). Cool. Freeze in syrup as described in Freezing section under Method 2. Store up to one year.

Elderberry Jelly

Follow recipe for Apple Jelly, but instead of apples, use 2kg (4lb) elderberries. Cook with 575ml (1pt) water. Continue as directed in Jelly section, allowing 350g (12oz) sugar to every 575ml (1pt) juice.

Elderberries, Stewed and Frozen

Treat exactly as Fruit, Stewed and Frozen – see appropriate entry.

Elderberry Syrup

See section on Fruit Syrups.
Make by Method 1 or 2, adding *no* water but the juice of 1 medium lemon. Allow 350g (12oz) sugar to every 575ml (1pt) strained fruit juice.

Elderflower and Gooseberry Jam

See Gooseberry and Elderflower Jam.

F

Fig and Apple Jam

For a yield of about 1¾kg (3½lb):
Coarsely mince ½kg (1lb) dried figs (remove stalks first) with 1½kg (3lb) peeled and cored cooking apples. Put into large pan with ¾ litre (1½pt) water, juice of 2 small lemons and 1 level teaspoon mixed spice. Simmer until fruit is thick, pulpy and very soft and contents of pan reduced by at least half. Stir in 1¼kg (2½lb) sugar. Continue as directed in Jam section.

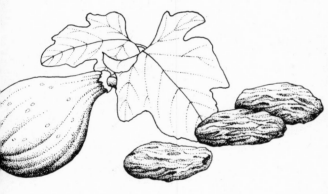

Figs in Alcohol

See section on Fruits in Alcohol, with special reference to Figs in Whisky.

Figs, Bottled

Remove stems from fresh figs and peel. Pack into jars. Treat exactly as Tomatoes, Whole Bottled – see appropriate entry. Substitute water or syrup for brine.

Figs, Frozen

Wash and dry fresh fruit, cut off stems and peel. Leave whole or slice. Sprinkle generously with lemon juice. Freeze in syrup as described in Freezing section under Method 2. Store up to one year.

Fig and Rhubarb Jam

See Fig and Apple Jam, but substitute rhubarb for apples.

Five Fruit Marmalade

For a yield of 4½kg (10lb) use:
1½kg (3lb) mixed citrus fruit consisting of 1 grapefruit, 2 lemons, 1 lime, 1 orange and 2 mandarins (or clementines or satsumas), 3½ litres (6pt) water and 2¾kg (6lb) sugar. Choose the most convenient method, for personal requirements, from Nos 1 to 4.

French Beans, Salted

See section on Salting.

Fruit Pulp, Bottled

See section on Bottling, with particular reference to directions for processing fruit pulp on page 15.

Fruit, Stewed and Frozen

Cook fruit for stewing in the usual way, adding sugar, syrup or artificial sweetener to taste. Slightly undercook as fruit will soften somewhat during thawing. Pack into containers when cold. Seal and label. Store up to nine months. Thaw about two or three hours at kitchen temperature. Reheat gently or serve cold.

G

Gage Plums, Bottled

Stalk plums then wash and dry. Treat exactly as Cherries, Red and Black, Bottled – see appropriate entry. It is important to note that gage plums should *not* be bottled by Method 3 (slow oven).

Gherkins, Pickled

Soak required amount of well-washed gherkins in brine solution for 3 days. Drain and dry. Transfer to large glass, pottery or rigid plastic bowl. Cover with hot spiced vinegar. Cover securely (with plastic film, for example) and leave at kitchen temperature for 24 hours. Drain off vinegar, bring to boil and pour over gherkins. Cover. Leave for 24 hours. Repeat last process once more. Transfer gherkins to jars. Fill with vinegar in which gherkins were soaking, adding extra cold spiced vinegar if necessary. Cover. Leave for six to eight weeks before eating.

Ginger and Apple Jam

See Apple and Ginger Jam.

Ginger and Marrow Jam

See Marrow and Ginger Jam.

Ginger and Orange Marmalade

For a yield of 2¼kg (5lb), follow recipe for Seville Orange Marmalade but cut peel into short, stubby pieces to give 'chunky' effect. Add 50 to 75g (2 to 3oz) chopped preserved ginger with the sugar. If liked, deepen colour by adding 1 level tablespoon black treacle at the same time.

Ginger and Rhubarb Jam

See Rhubarb and Ginger Jam.

Gooseberries in Alcohol

See section on Fruits in Alcohol.

Gooseberries, Bottled (for Dessert use)

Top and tail gooseberries and make a nick in each to prevent shrivelling. Pack well down into jars then treat exactly as Blackberries, Bottled, but adjust methods as follows:

Method 1
Raise temperature to 82°C (180°F) and maintain ¼ hour.

Method 2
Same temperature as blackberries but maintain 10 minutes.

Method 3
Same temperature as blackberries but process ½ to 2kg (1 to 4lb) for 55 to 70 minutes; 2¼ to 4½kg (5 to 10lb) for 75 to 90 minutes.

Method 4
Same temperature as blackberries but process ½ to 2kg (1 to 4lb) for 40 to 50 minutes; 2¼ to 4½kg (5 to 10lb) for 55 to 70 minutes.

Method 5

Same process as for blackberries. Maintain pressure for 1 minute.

For Methods 1 and 2, allow extra time for large size jars as given at the end of blackberry entry.

Gooseberries, Bottled (for pies etc)

Top and tail gooseberries then make a nick in each to prevent shrivelling. Treat exactly as Blackberries, Bottled – see appropriate entry.

Gooseberry and Cherry Jam

See Gooseberry Jam. Use 1kg (2lb) gooseberries and ½kg (1lb) stoned dessert cherries, weighed *after* stoning. Keep amounts of water and sugar the same.

Gooseberry Chutney

Follow recipe for Apple Chutney, but instead of apples, use 2kg (4lb) topped and tailed cooking gooseberries and the finely shredded peel of both 1 large, well-washed lemon and 1 orange.

Gooseberry and Elderflower Jam

See Gooseberry Jam. Make in exactly the same way but add 12 elderflower heads (tied in a muslin bag) at the same time as the sugar. Make sure the flowers are minus stalks. Remove the bag after setting point has been reached.

Note: The elderflower heads add a note of subtlety to the jam.

Gooseberry Jam

For a yield of 2¼kg (5lb) use:
1½kg (3lb) gooseberries, 575ml (1pt) water and 1½kg (3lb) sugar. For instructions see Jam section.

Note: After boiling with sugar, gooseberry jam is inclined to turn pink. If cooked in a copper pan it will, however, stay green.

Gooseberry Jelly

Follow recipe for Apple Jelly, but instead of apples, use 2kg (4lb) topped and tailed cooking gooseberries.

Gooseberry and Loganberry Jam

See Gooseberry Jam. Use half gooseberries and half loganberries. Reduce water to 150ml (¼pt). Keep amount of sugar the same.

Gooseberries, Pulped and Frozen

See section on Freezing with particular reference to Fruit Purées. Follow Method 2, using topped and tailed gooseberries and, if liked, a small amount of grated lemon peel. Store up to one year.

Gooseberry and Raspberry Jam

See Raspberry Jam. Use half raspberries, half topped and tailed gooseberries and 150ml (¼pt) water. Keep amount of sugar the same.

Gooseberry and Raspberry Syrup

See section on Fruit Syrups. Make by Methods 1 or 2, adding *no* water. Allow 350g (12oz) sugar to every 575ml (1pt) strained fruit juice.

Gooseberries, Stewed and Frozen

See section on Freezing. Treat exactly as Fruit, Stewed and Frozen – see appropriate entry.

Gooseberry and Strawberry Jam

See Gooseberry Jam. Use half gooseberries and half strawberries. Reduce water to 150ml (¼pt). Keep amount of sugar the same.

Gooseberry and Strawberry Jelly

Follow recipe for Apple Jelly but instead of apples, use 1kg (2lb) gooseberries and 1kg (2lb) strawberries.

Gooseberry and Strawberry Syrup

See section on Fruit Syrups. Make by Method 1 or 2, adding *no* water. Allow 350g (12oz) sugar to every 575ml (1pt) strained fruit juice.

Grapefruit, Bottled

Peel grapefruit, removing all traces of pith. Either cut into slices or remove half-moon shaped segments of fruit by cutting in between membranes. Treat exactly as Cherries, Red and Black, Bottled – see appropriate entry. It is important to note that grapefruit should *not* be bottled by Method 3 (slow oven).

Note: Discard pips before packing into jars.

Grapefruit, Frozen

Peel grapefruit, removing all traces of pith. Cut into segments which are completely free from skin and pips. Either freeze without sugar, or proceed as described in Method 3, waiting for the sugar to dissolve before freezing. Store up to one year.

Grapefruit and Lemon Jelly Marmalade

Follow recipe and method for Jelly Marmalade on page 65. Instead of Seville oranges, use 2 grapefruit and 2 lemons to give total weight of 1kg (2lb).

Grapefruit Marmalade

See section on Marmalade. For a yield of 2¼kg (5lb) use:

¾kg (1½lb) grapefruit, 1¾ litres (3pt) water, 3 level teaspoons citric or tartaric acid (available from pharmacies) and 1½kg (3lb) sugar. Choose the most convenient method, for personal requirements, from Nos 1 to 4.

Grapefruit Peel

See section on Candied Peel.

Grapes, Frozen

Choose whole seedless grapes. Otherwise halve large grapes and remove pips. Sprinkle with lemon juice. Freeze in syrup as described under Method 2. Store up to one year.

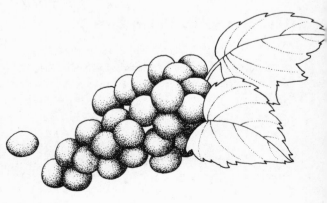

Greengages in Alcohol

See section on Fruits in Alcohol, and the Rum Pot in particular.

Greengages, Bottled

Stalk greengages then wash and dry. Treat exactly as Cherries, Red and Black, Bottled – see appropriate entry.

It is important to note that greengages should *not* be bottled by Method 3 (slow oven).

Greengages, Frozen

Choose slightly under-ripe gages. Halve and remove stones. Toss with lemon juice. Freeze in syrup as described under Method 2. Store up to one year.

If gages are unstoned, treat exactly as above but store no longer than six months.

On thawing, the fruit will appear very soft.

Greengage Jam

For a yield of 2¼kg (5lb) use:
1½kg (3lb) slightly under-ripe greengages, 275ml (½pt) water and 1½kg (3lb) sugar. For instructions, see Jam section.

Greengages, Pulped and Frozen

See section on Freezing with particular reference to Fruit Purées. Follow Method 2, using stoned and halved fruit. Store up to one year.

Greengages, Stewed and Frozen

Treat exactly as Fruit, Stewed and Frozen – see appropriate entry.

Green Pepper and Red Tomato Chutney

Follow recipe for Apple Chutney, but instead of apples only, use 2¼kg (5lb) skinned tomatoes, 2 large, de-seeded green peppers, ½kg (1lb) apples and 1 tube (about 175g or 6oz) tomato purée to heighten colour. Tomatoes should be chopped but not minced.

Green Pepper and Red Tomato Sauce

Make up Red Tomato and Green Pepper Chutney then continue as directed for Sauces.

Green Tomato Chutney

Follow recipe for Apple Chutney, but instead of apples, use coarsely minced green tomatoes.

Green Tomatoes, Pickled

Dissolve ½kg (1lb) granulated or preserving sugar in 275ml (½pt) spiced vinegar. Bring to the boil. Add 1kg (2lb) small green tomatoes. Simmer just long enough to cook the fruit. (It is quite usual for the skins to split.) Avoid overcooking or the tomatoes will disintegrate. Drain. Pack fruit into bottles. Boil sweetened syrup with 1 or 2 peeled garlic cloves until thick and syrupy. Pour over fruit, cover while hot.

H

Herbs

See section on Drying.

Herbs, Frozen

See section on Freezing, with particular reference to herbs. Follow either Method 1 or 2, depending on which is the most convenient. Store up to one year.

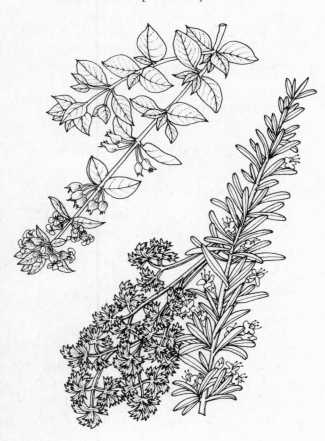

Hotch Potch Chutney

Follow recipe for Apple Chutney, but instead of apples, use ½kg (1lb) *each*, tomatoes, mushrooms, sliced runner beans and diced marrow.

J

Japonica Jam

The fruit of the Japonica tree is similar to Quince. To make, follow recipe for Rose Hip Jam. Wash the fruit well but do not peel or core. Cut into pieces and simmer until very soft in water, allowing 1¾ litres (3pt) to every 1kg (2lb) fruit. Strain. Weigh pulp. Cook with an equal weight of sugar. If liked, flavour with powdered ginger, cinnamon or allspice, adding it at the same time as the sugar.

K

Kale, Frozen

See Curly Kale.

Kiwi Fruit, Bottled

Peel Kiwi Fruit and slice. Pack into jars. Treat exactly as Cherries, Red and Black, Bottled – see appropriate entry.

It is important to note two things: the fruits should *not* be bottled by Method 3, and syrup is a better choice than water.

Kiwi Fruit, Frozen

Peel and slice fruit. Sprinkle with lemon juice. Freeze in syrup as described under Method 2. Store up to six months.

Kohlrabi, Frozen

Peel turnip-shaped, small-sized Kohlrabi and cut into dice. Blanch 2 minutes. Freeze in polythene bags or containers. Store up to one year.

L

Leeks, Frozen

Choose medium-sized leeks. Trim, wash thoroughly and slice. Blanch 1 minute. Freeze in polythene bags or containers. Store up to six months. For whole leeks, use young and tender ones. Trim and wash thoroughly. Blanch 3 minutes. Pack into containers, heads to tails. Freeze up to six months.

Lemon Apple Jelly

Follow recipe for Apple Jelly but, when simmering, add peel of 2 lemons, cut into strips.

Lemons, Bottled

Peel lemons, removing all traces of pith. Cut into thinnish slices. Treat exactly as Cherries, Red and Black, Bottled – see appropriate entry. It is important to note that lemons should *not* be bottled by Method 3 (slow oven).

Note: Discard pips before packing into jars.

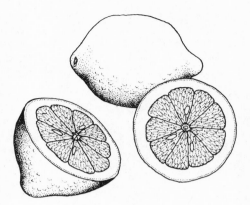

Lemon Curd

See section on Fruit Curds.

Lemons, Frozen

Wash and dry. Pack into containers and freeze whole. Store up to one year.

Lemon and Grapefruit Jelly Marmalade

Follow recipe and method for Jelly Marmalade on page 65. Instead of Seville oranges, use 2 grapefruit and 2 lemons to give total weight of 1kg (2lb).

Lemon Juice, Frozen

Squeeze required number of lemons. Strain juice. Transfer to small containers, leaving 1¼cm (½in) headroom for expansion. Cover and label. Store up to one year.

Alternatively, freeze juice in ice cube tray fitted with dividers. When completely hard, transfer to plastic bags and store up to one year.

Lemon and Lime Marmalade

For a yield of 2¼kg (5lb) use:
350g (12oz) lemons, 350g (12oz) limes, 1¾ litres (3pt) water and 1½kg (3lb) sugar. Choose the most convenient method, for personal requirements, from Nos 1 to 4.

Lemon and Mandarin Jelly Marmalade

Follow recipe and method for Jelly Marmalade on page 65. Instead of Seville oranges, use ½kg (1lb) lemons, 1 large sweet orange (225g or 8oz) and 225g (8oz) mandarins. Use *all* the mandarin peel in the marmalade plus half that of the other two fruits.

Lemon Marmalade

For a yield of 2¼kg (5lb) use:
¾kg (1½lb) lemons, 1¾ litres (3pt) water and 1½kg (3lb) sugar. Choose the most convenient method, for personal requirements, from Nos 1 to 4.

Lemon and Orange Marmalade

For a yield of 2¼kg (5lb) use:
350g (12oz) sweet oranges, 350g (12oz) lemons, 1¾ litres (3pt) water and 1½kg (3lb) sugar. Choose the most convenient method, for personal requirements, from Nos 1 to 4.

Lemon Peel

See section on Candied Peel.

Lemon Peel, Frozen

Wash and dry blemish-free lemons. Grate off peel finely. Transfer to small, airtight containers. Freeze up to six months.

Lemon and Rhubarb Jam

See Rhubarb and Ginger Jam. Instead of ginger, add the finely grated peel of 2 lemons to the ingredients in the pan before bringing to the boil.

Lemon Slices, Frozen

If slices are required for garnishing dishes or adding to drinks, 'open freeze' by standing on trays lined with cling film (*not* foil). When hard, layer into suitable containers with interleaving sheets between each layer. Cover and label. Store up to one year.

For sweet lemon slices, pack into containers, sprinkling sugar between each layer. Leave until sugar dissolves before freezing. Store up to one year.

Lemon Syrup

See section on Fruit Syrups with special instructions for Lemon Syrup.

Lime and Clementine Marmalade

For a yield of 2¼kg (5lb) use:
½kg (1lb) limes, 225g (8oz) clementines, 1¾ litres (3pt) water and 1½kg (3lb) sugar. Choose the most convenient method, for personal requirements, from Nos 1 to 4.

Lime and Lemon Marmalade

For a yield of 2¼kg (5lb) use:
350g (12oz) lemons, 350g (12oz) limes, 1¾ litres (3pt) water and 1½kg (3lb) sugar. Choose the most convenient method, for personal requirements, from Nos 1 to 4 in Marmalade section.

Lime Marmalade

Made identically to Lemon Marmalade – see appropriate entry.

Lime and Orange Marmalade

For a yield of 2¼kg (5lb) use:
350g (12oz) sweet oranges, 350g (12oz) limes, 1¾ litres (3pt) water and 1½kg (3lb) sugar. Choose the most convenient method, for personal requirements, from Nos 1 to 4 in Marmalade section.

Lime Peel

See section on Candied Peel.

Loganberries in Alcohol

See section on Fruits in Alcohol.

Loganberries, Bottled

Hull fruit and remove any that are showing signs of mildew. Treat exactly as Blackberries, Bottled – see appropriate entry.

Loganberries, Frozen

Choose ripe fruit in prime condition. Freeze, following either Methods 1, 2 or 3 depending on personal requirements. Store up to one year.

Loganberry and Gooseberry Jam

See Gooseberry Jam. Use half gooseberries and half loganberries. Reduce water to 150ml (¼pt). Keep sugar the same.

Loganberry Jam

For a yield of 2¼kg (5lb) use:
1½kg (3lb) freshly picked loganberries and 1½kg (3lb) sugar. Put berries into pan. Crush over medium heat until juice runs. Gently bring to boil. Add sugar. Stir until dissolved. Boil briskly until set. For further instructions, see Jam section.

Loganberry (Frozen) Jam

Read Freezer Jams in Jam section on page 54. For a yield of about 1½kg (3lb) use:
550g (1¼lb) ripe loganberries, 2 tablespoons lemon juice, 1kg (2lb) caster sugar, ½ bottle (4 fl oz or 125ml) liquid pectin.

Loganberry Jelly

Follow recipe for Apple Jelly, but instead of apples, use 2kg (4lb) loganberries. Simmer fruit with 575ml (1pt) water and the juice of 2 medium lemons.

Loganberry Syrup

See section on Fruit Syrups. Make by Methods 1 or 2, adding *no* water. Allow 350g (12oz) sugar to every 575ml (1pt) strained fruit juice.

M

Mandarin and Apricot (Dried) Jam

See Apricot (dried) and Mandarin Jam.

Mandarin and Lemon Jelly Marmalade

Follow recipe and method for Jelly Marmalade on page 65. Instead of Seville oranges, use ½kg (1lb) lemons, 1 large sweet orange (225g or 8oz) and 225g (8oz) mandarins. Use *all* the mandarin peel in the marmalade plus half that of the other two fruits.

Mange Tout, Frozen

As peas and pods are cooked and eaten together, choose young mange tout and blanch 2 minutes. Freeze in polythene bags or containers. Store up to one year.

Mango Chutney (West African)

Dissolve ½kg (1lb) soft brown sugar in 575ml (1pt) vinegar. Add ½kg (1lb) mixed dried fruit (but no peel), 50g (2oz) powdered ginger, ½ level teaspoon cayenne pepper, 3 to 4 level teaspoons salt, 25g (1oz) peeled and sliced garlic and 2kg (4lb) green mangoes peeled and diced. Simmer 1½ to 2 hours or until chutney is of jam-like consistency.

Mango Sauce

Make up Mango Chutney then continue as directed for Sauces.

Marmalade, 'Vintage' Style

Follow recipe for Seville Orange Marmalade, adding 1 level tablespoon black treacle with the sugar.

Marrow and Apple Chutney

Follow recipe for Apple Chutney, but use 1kg (2lb) apples and 1kg (2lb) de-rinded, de-seeded and cubed marrow.

Marrow, Frozen

Choose young marrows. Peel, slice into rings and remove seeds. Cut flesh into 1¼cm (½in) cubes. Blanch 3 minutes. Freeze in polythene bags or containers. Store up to six months.

Marrow and Ginger Jam

For a yield of 2¼kg (5lb), use:
1½kg (3lb) marrow (peeled and de-seeded weight), the finely grated peel and juice of 4 medium lemons, 50 to 75g (2 to 3oz) root ginger lightly tapped with a hammer to bruise it, and 1½kg (3lb) sugar.

Cube marrow and steam gently until tender. Transfer to bowl. Stir in all remaining ingredients. Cover. Leave to stand 24 hours. Transfer to preserving pan. Heat slowly until sugar dissolves, stirring. Bring to boil and boil fairly briskly until pieces of marrow are transparent and syrup is thick. Test for setting by methods described in Jam section but bear in mind that Marrow Jam never sets firmly and is more like a Continental conserve than a jam.

Marrow, Pickled

Layer 1kg (2lb) diced marrow in bowl with 125g (4oz) salt. Leave overnight. Drain and rinse. Transfer to saucepan. Add about 425ml (¾pt) spiced vinegar. Simmer gently, covered, until marrow is just tender. Transfer both marrow and hot vinegar to jars. Cover when cold.

Medlar Butter

See sections on Fruit Cheeses and Butters.

Medlar Cheese

Golden brown and like large rose hips in shape, Medlars are hard to obtain these days and are found growing only occasionally. To make cheese, see section on Fruit Cheeses. Cut up medlars (which have been left a couple of weeks after picking to soften; even longer if very hard) and simmer in water until very soft and pulpy. The finely grated peel and juice of 1 large lemon may be added to every ½kg (1lb) fruit.

Melon, Frozen

Choose a ripe melon and cut flesh into cubes. Alternatively, scoop into small balls with melon scoop. Freeze in syrup as described under Method 2 in Freezing section. Store up to six months.

Mint Jelly

Cut up 2kg (4lb) green apples and simmer until soft and pulpy in 575ml (1pt) water.

Add 275ml (½pt) vinegar. Simmer 5 more minutes. Strain. Allow ½kg (1lb) sugar to every 575ml (1pt) juice. Dissolve sugar in juice over low heat. Boil briskly for 5 minutes. Add finely chopped fresh mint to taste. Continue to boil until setting point is reached. Leave until a thin skin forms on top. Stir round. Pot and cover as directed in Jelly section.

Note: For a more distinctive colour, tint with green food-colouring when adding the chopped mint.

For a clear jelly, add sprigs of mint after jelly has been boiling briskly for 5 minutes. Remove as soon as setting point is reached.

Mixed Fruit Marmalade

For a yield of 2¼kg (5lb) use:
¾kg (1½lb) mixed citrus fruit consisting of 1 grapefruit, 2 lemons and 1 or 2 sweet oranges. Also 1¾ litres (3pt) water and 1½kg (3lb) sugar. Choose the most convenient method, for personal requirements, from Nos 1 to 4 in Marmalade section.

Mixed Pickles

For Mixed Pickles, choose a selection of cauliflower, pickling onions or shallots, gherkins or thick slices of unpeeled cucumber and dwarf or French beans which have been topped, tailed and snapped in half.

Break cauliflower into florets and put into a brine solution with the skinned onions or shallots, gherkins or cucumber and the beans. Leave for 48 hours. Drain and rinse. Pack into jars. Fill with cold spiced vinegar. Cover. Leave about six to eight weeks before eating.

Mixed Soft Fruits, Bottled

Choose 2 or 3 soft fruits, treat according to type and bottle together exactly as described for Blackberries, Bottled – see appropriate entry.

Morello Cherries in Alcohol

See section on Fruits in Alcohol, with special reference to the Rum Pot and Cherries in Brandy.

Morello Cherries, Frozen

Treat exactly as Cherries, Frozen – see appropriate entry. When thawed, use fruit in pies, crumbles etc. Store up to one year.

Morello Cherry Jam

See Cherry Jam. Use half quantity of lemon juice. Otherwise keep all ingredients the same.

Morello Cherries, Pickled

Follow recipe for Blackberries, Pickled, but use 1kg (2lb) stoned Morello cherries instead of blackberries. Simmer in the sweetened vinegar until tender. Continue as directed in blackberry recipe.

Mulberry and Apple Jelly

Follow recipe for Apple Jelly, but instead of apples only, use 1kg (2lb) cooking apples and 1kg (2lb) mulberries.

Mulberry and Blackberry Jam

See Blackberry Jam. Use half mulberries and half blackberries. Keep the amounts of sugar, lemon juice and water the same.

Mulberry and Blackberry Syrup

See section on Fruit Syrups. Make by Methods 1 or 2, adding *no* water. Allow 350g (12oz) sugar to every 575ml (1pt) strained fruit juice.

Mulberries, Bottled

Carefully pick over mulberries, discarding any that are mildewed. Treat exactly as Blackberries, Bottled – see appropriate entry.

Mulberries, Frozen

Choose dark red and ripe mulberries in prime condition. Freeze in syrup as described under Method 2. Store up to one year.

Mulberries, Stewed and Frozen

Treat exactly as Fruit, Stewed and Frozen – see appropriate entry.

Mulberry Syrup

See section on Fruit Syrups. Make by Method 1 or 2, adding *no* water but the juice of 1 medium lemon. Allow 350g (12oz) sugar to every 575ml (1pt) strained fruit juice.

Mushrooms, Dried

See section on drying.

Mushrooms, Frozen

As cultivated mushrooms are available throughout the year, there is no point in freezing them. However, fragrant field mushrooms are worth keeping. Pick young mushrooms. Trim stalks and wash *very* well. Pack into containers while damp. Alternatively, fry lightly in butter or oil and pack. Do not blanch as this causes toughness. Store up to three months.

Mushrooms, Pickled

Trim ½kg (1lb) button mushrooms. Put into saucepan with just enough cider vinegar to cover. Add 1 small peeled and grated onion, 1 small bay leaf, ¼ level teaspoon grated nutmeg, 1 level teaspoon salt, 1 level teaspoon ground ginger and 2 or 3 drops Tabasco.

Cook slowly, covered, until mushrooms have shrunk considerably – about 10 to 15 minutes. Pack mushrooms into jars and top up with hot vinegar and spices. Cover. Leave for about one week before eating.

Mustard Pickles, Hot

Follow recipe for Piccalilli, Hot.

Mustard Pickles, Mild

Follow recipe for Piccalilli, Mild.

N

Nectarines, Frozen

See Peaches, Frozen.

Nectarines, Halved and Bottled

Blanch nectarines by covering with boiling water. Leave 1 minute. Drain. Cover with cold water. Leave until cool enough to handle then slide off skins. Halve nectarines, remove stones and pack fruit into jars. Treat exactly as Blackberries, Bottled, but adjust methods as follows:

Method 1
Raise temperature to 82°C (180°F) and maintain ¼ hour.

Method 2
Same temperature as blackberries but maintain 20 minutes.

Method 3
Not recommended.

Method 4
Same temperature as blackberries but process ½ to 2kg (1 to 4lb) for 50 to 60 minutes; 2¼ to 4½kg (5 to 10lb) for 65 to 80 minutes.

Method 5
Same process as blackberries but maintain pressure for 3 to 4 minutes.

For Methods 1 and 2 allow extra time for large size jars as given at the end of blackberry entry.

Nectarines, Pulped and Frozen

See Peaches, Pulped and Frozen.

Nectarines, Stewed and Frozen

See Peaches, Stewed and Frozen.

O

Onions, Frozen

Peel and chop onions. (Pieces should not be too small). Blanch 2 minutes. Freeze in polythene bags or containers. Store up to three months. Use in cooked dishes *only*.

Onions, Pickled

Skin required amount of onions. Put into bowl. Cover completely with brine. Keep onions immersed by covering with plate weighed down with heavy garden stone. Leave 36 hours. Drain. Rinse. Drain thoroughly again. Pack into jars. Fill with cold spiced vinegar. Cover. Leave about two to three months before eating.

Orange and Apple Jam

See Apple and Orange Jam.

Oranges, Bottled

Peel oranges, removing all traces of pith. Either cut into slices or remove half-moon shaped segments of fruit by cutting in between membranes. Treat exactly as

Cherries, Red and Black, Bottled – see appropriate entry.

It is important to note that oranges should *not* be bottled by Method 3 (slow oven).

Note: Discard pips before packing into jars.

Orchard Chutney

Follow recipe for Apple Chutney, but instead of apples, use ½kg (1lb) *each*, apples, plums, pears and blackberries.

Orange and Cranberry Jam

See Cranberry and Orange Jam.

Oranges, Frozen

Treat exactly as grapefruit – see appropriate entry.

Orange and Ginger Marmalade

For a yield of 2¼kg (5lb) follow recipe for Seville Orange Marmalade but cut peel into short, stubby pieces to give 'chunky' effect. Add 50 to 75g (2 to 3oz) chopped preserved ginger with the sugar. If liked, deepen colour by adding 1 level tablespoon black treacle at the same time.

Orange Jelly Marmalade

Follow recipe and Method for Jelly Marmalade on page 65.

Orange and Lemon Marmalade

For a yield of 2¼kg (5lb) use:
350g (12oz) sweet oranges, 350g (12oz) lemons, 1¾ litres (3pt) water and 1½kg (3lb) sugar. Choose the most convenient method, for personal requirements, from Nos 1 to 4.

Orange and Lime Marmalade

For a yield of 2¼kg (5lb) use:
350g (12oz) sweet oranges, 350g (12oz) limes, 1¾ litres (3pt) water and 1½kg (3lb) sugar. Choose the most convenient method, for personal requirements, from Nos 1 to 4.

Orange Marmalade (Sweet Oranges)

For a yield of 2¼kg (5lb) use:
¾kg (1½lb) sweet oranges, 1¾ litres (3pt) water, juice of 3 large lemons and 1½kg (3lb) sugar. Choose the most convenient method, for personal requirements, from Nos 1 to 4.

Note: If preferred, use 3 level teaspoons citric or tartaric acid instead of the lemon juice. It is available from pharmacies.

Orange Peel, Candied

See section on Candied Peel.

Orange Peel, Frozen

Treat exactly as Lemon Peel, Frozen – see appropriate entry.

Oranges, Pickled

Follow recipe for Blackberries, Pickled, but use 1kg (2lb) washed, dried and *unpeeled* oranges cut into slices of average thickness. Simmer in the sweetened vinegar until the peel is tender, keeping heat very low. Continue as directed in blackberry recipe. For an exotic flavour, add 2 cardamom seeds, 2 cloves, 1 blade mace and a small piece of bay leaf to every jar before filling with cooked down, sweetened vinegar.

Orange and Rhubarb Chutney

Follow recipe for Apple Chutney but instead of apples, use 1½kg (3lb) rhubarb (trimmed weight) and ½kg (1lb) oranges which should be washed well, dried, left unpeeled and cubed. All pips should be discarded.

Note: This is a deliciously flavoured chutney and teams well with duck, goose, game and pork.

Orange and Rhubarb Sauce

Make up Orange and Rhubarb Chutney then continue as directed for Sauces.

Orange Syrup

See section on Fruit Syrups with special instructions for Orange Syrup.

P

Parsley, Dried

Blanch bunches of parsley by dipping in boiling water for 1 minute. This preserves its bright green colour. Tie the stems loosely into bundles then tie the bundles on to oven racks so that they actually hang in the oven. Heat at 120°C (250°F) Gas ½, for 1 hour. Switch off the heat. Leave parsley where it is until oven has cooled down completely and the parsley itself is very crisp. If still soft, switch on the oven again, cook a further ¼ to ½ hour and leave in the oven until dried and very crisp. Crush with a rolling pin and store in containers with airtight stoppers.

Parsnips, Frozen

Choose medium-sized and young parsnips. Peel and cut into dice. Blanch 2 minutes. Freeze in polythene bags or containers. Store up to one year.

Note: Parsnip dice and carrot dice may be frozen together.

Peaches in Alcohol

See section on Fruits in Alcohol with special reference to the Rum Pot and Peaches in Brandy.

Peach and Apricot Chutney

Follow recipe for Apple Chutney but instead of apples, use 1kg (2lb) skinned fresh peaches and 1kg (2lb) skinned fresh apricots. Cut both into chunks.

Note: To skin fruit, cover with boiling water and leave 1 minute. Drain. Cover with cold water. Leave 1 minute. Slide off skins.

Peach and Apricot Sauce

Make up Apricot and Peach Chutney then continue as directed for Sauces.

Peaches in Brandy

See section on Fruits in Alcohol.

Peaches, Dried

See Apples and Apricots, Dried. Also read section on Drying. Treat exactly as Apricots, Dried, but allow a little longer for drying, as the fruit halves are larger. Do not peel peaches but cut in half and remove stones. The peach halves are ready when they feel firm and hard.

Peaches, Frozen

Skin peaches by covering with boiling water, leaving for 1 minute, draining and then covering with cold water. When cool enough to handle, slide off skins and either halve peaches or cut into slices. Sprinkle with lemon juice. Freeze in syrup as described under Method 2. Store up to one year.

Peaches, Halved and Bottled

Blanch peaches by covering with boiling water. Leave 1 minute. Drain. Cover with cold water. Leave until cool enough to handle then slide off skins. Halve peaches, remove stones and pack fruit into jars. Treat exactly as Blackberries, Bottled, but adjust methods as follows:

Method 1
Raise temperature to 82°C (180°F) and maintain ¼ hour.

Method 2
Same temperature as blackberries but maintain 20 minutes.

Method 3
Not recommended.

Method 4
Same temperature as blackberries but process ½ to 2kg (1 to 4lb) for 50 to 60 minutes; 2¼ to 4½kg (5 to 10lb) for 65 to 80 minutes.

Method 5
Same process as blackberries but maintain pressure for 3 to 4 minutes.

For Methods 1 and 2, allow extra time for large size jars as given at end of blackberry entry.

Peach Jam

For a yield of about 2¼kg (5lb) use:
1¾kg (3½lb) peaches (just ripe; not over-ripe), juice of 2 large lemons, 275ml (½pt) water and 1½kg (3lb) sugar.

Blanch peaches by covering for 1 minute with boiling water, draining and covering with cold water. When cool enough to handle, slide off skins and cut peaches into quarters. Cook as directed in Jam section until jam sets and the fruit is clear and the liquid deepish gold.

Peaches, Pickled

Simmer 2kg (4lb) skinned, stoned and quartered peaches in about ¾ litre (1½pt) spiced vinegar until just tender. Pack fruit into jars. Fill with hot vinegar. Cover.

Leave three to four months before eating.

Note: For a subtle flavour, add a few cardamom seeds and some strips of orange peel to each jar.

Peach and Plum Jam

See Plum Jam. Use 1kg (2lb) cooking plums and ½kg (1lb) slightly under-ripe and skinned peaches. To skin peaches, cover with boiling water and leave about 1 minute. Transfer to bowl of cold water. Drain. Remove skin. Cut up flesh with a stainless knife.

Peaches, Pulped and Frozen

See section on Freezing with particular reference to Fruit Purées. Follow either Methods 1 or 2, using skinned peaches. (For skinning instructions, see entry on Peaches, Frozen.) Store up to one year.

Peaches, Stewed and Frozen

Treat exactly as Fruit, Stewed and Frozen – see appropriate entry.

Peaches, Sweet-Sour

Follow recipe for Pears, Sweet-Sour. Peaches should be blanched, so cover with boiling water, leave for 1 minute and drain. Cover with cold water and leave 1 or 2 minutes. Slide off skins, halve peaches and remove stones. Cut halves into thickish slices before simmering.

Pears in Alcohol

See section on Fruits in Alcohol, and the Rum Pot in particular.

Pears, Cooking, Bottled

Peel pears, cut into eighths and remove cores. Stew gently, but *do not allow* to break up. Pack into jars then treat exactly as Tomatoes, Whole Bottled. Substitute water or syrup for brine. *Do not* process by Method 3.

Pears, Dessert, Bottled

Peel pears, cut into eighths and remove cores. To prevent excessive browning, drop into salt water made by dissolving 25g (1oz) salt in 2½ litres (4pt) water. Drain and rinse. Pack into jars. Treat exactly as Tomatoes, Whole Bottled – see appropriate entry. Substitute water or syrup for brine. *Do not* process by Method 3.

Pears, Dessert and Frozen

Choose pears in prime condition. Peel, quarter and core but slice if very large. Sprinkle with lemon juice. Freeze in syrup as described under Method 2. Freeze up to one year.

Pears, Dried

See Apples, Dried. Also read section on Drying. Choose firm dessert pears. Peel, cut into eighths and remove cores and blemishes. Drop into salt water as apples. Leave 5 minutes. Drain. Arrange on trays. Allow about 5 to 8 hours drying time if the process is continuous, or a period of 3 to 4 days if the heat is intermittent. The pears are ready when they look similar to the apples.

Pears, Pickled

Simmer 2kg (4lb) peeled, quartered and cored pears in about ¾ litre (1½pt) spiced vinegar until just tender. Pack fruit into jars with, if liked, some fresh mint leaves. Fill with hot vinegar. Cover. Leave three to four months before eating.

Pear and Pineapple Chutney

Follow recipe for Apple Chutney but instead of apples, use 1kg (2lb) cooking pears and 1kg (2lb) diced, fresh pineapple (prepared weight). Do not include the centre core of the pineapple which will remain rather tough.

Pear and Prune Chutney

Follow recipe for Apple Chutney but instead of apples, use ½kg (1lb) pitted prunes and 1½kg (3lb) cooking pears.

Pear and Prune Sauce

Make up Pear and Prune Chutney then continue as directed for Sauces.

Pears, Pulped and Frozen

See section on Freezing with particular reference to Fruit Purées. Follow Method 1 for ripe dessert pears; Method 2 for cooking pears, adding a little lemon juice to the water. Freeze up to one year.

Pears, Stewed and Frozen

Treat exactly as Fruit, Stewed and Frozen – see appropriate entry. Cooking pears are better than dessert pears for stewing. If adding cloves, do so cautiously as the flavour intensifies during freezing.

Pears, Sweet-Sour

In large saucepan, dissolve 1kg (2lb) granulated or preserving sugar in 575ml (1pt) cider vinegar. Add large muslin bag containing strips of lemon peel (cut from 1 small lemon), 1 level tablespoon mixed pickling spice, 1 cinnamon stick and 6 cloves. Add 2kg (4lb) cooking pears which should be peeled, quartered and cored.

Simmer gently until fruit is just tender; do not overcook or pears may disintegrate. Keep pan covered throughout. Strain off syrup. Pack fruit neatly and carefully into jars. Fill with hot syrup, boiled down until fairly thick and syrupy. Cover. Leave three to four months before eating.

Note: Keep a reserve of spare sweetened vinegar to hand. This is useful for topping up jars during storage as the fruit tends to absorb a substantial amount of syrup, and contents therefore shrink.

Peas, Frozen

Choose tender young peas and remove from pods. Blanch 1 to 2 minutes, depending on size. Freeze in polythene bags or containers. For peas which stay separate during storage, follow 'Free Flow' method of freezing described on page 29.

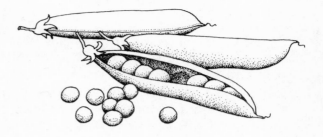

Note: Peas and carrot dice may be frozen together.

Peel, Mixed and Chopped

See section on Mincemeat.

Peppers, Frozen

Choose young, medium-sized peppers. Wash and dry them, leave whole and unblanched (the colour will stay brighter) then pack into containers and store up to six months.

Alternatively, halve and de-seed peppers and blanch 3 minutes. Freeze in polythene bags or containers. Store up to one year.

Piccalilli, Hot

Follow recipe for Piccalilli, Mild, until the brining stage, then continue as follows: Leave 24 hours. Drain and rinse vegetables. Leave on one side temporarily. Mix 15g (½oz) turmeric, 40g (1½oz) ground ginger, 40g (1½oz) dry mustard, 1½ level tablespoons flour and 175g (6oz) caster sugar to a smooth liquid with 575ml (1pt) distilled vinegar.

Pour a further 575ml (1pt) distilled vinegar into saucepan. Add prepared vegetables. Simmer until tender but still crisp. Stir in flour mixture. Cook, stirring continuously, until pickles come to boil and thicken. Simmer 3 minutes. Pack into jars. Cover when cold.

Piccalilli, Mild

Choose a selection of diced and unpeeled cucumber, diced marrow, skinned pickling onions, prepared green beans (topped, tailed, side strings removed then beans halved or sliced), cauliflower florets and small green tomatoes. *The total weight should be $2\frac{3}{4}$kg (6lb).* Cover vegetables with brine and leave 24 hours. Drain and rinse. Leave on one side.

Mix $1\frac{1}{2}$ level tablespoons dry mustard, 2 level teaspoons ground ginger, 40g ($1\frac{1}{2}$oz) flour, 15g ($\frac{1}{4}$oz) turmeric and 225g (8oz) caster sugar to a smooth liquid with $\frac{3}{4}$ litre ($1\frac{1}{2}$pt) distilled vinegar. Pour a further $\frac{3}{4}$ litre ($1\frac{1}{2}$pt) distilled vinegar into saucepan. Add prepared vegetables. Simmer until tender but still crisp. Stir in flour mixture. Cook, stirring continuously, until pickles come to boil and thicken. Simmer 3 minutes. Pack into jars. Cover when cold.

Pineapple in Alcohol

See section on Fruits in Alcohol, and the Rum Pot in particular.

Pineapple, Bottled

Skin pineapple with sharp knife and take out brown 'eyes' with apple corer. Cut into $2\frac{1}{2}$cm (1in) thick slices. Remove centre cores. Cut flesh into triangular segments. Pack into jars. Treat exactly as Blackberries, Bottled, but adjust methods as follows:

Method 1
Raise temperature to 82°C (180°F) and maintain $\frac{1}{4}$ hour.

Method 2
Same temperature as blackberries but maintain 20 minutes.

Method 3
Not recommended.

Method 4
Same as blackberries but process $\frac{1}{2}$ to 2kg (1 to 4lb) for 50 to 60 minutes; $2\frac{1}{4}$ to $4\frac{1}{2}$kg (5 to 10lb) for 65 to 80 minutes.

Method 5
Same process as blackberries but maintain pressure for 3 to 4 minutes.

For Methods 1 and 2, allow extra time for large size jars as given at end of blackberry entry.

Pineapple, Frozen

Skin pineapple and remove brown 'eyes' with apple corer. Cut into slices and remove centre core. Divide flesh into small segments. Freeze in syrup as described under Method 2. Store up to three months.

Pineapple and Pear Chutney

Follow recipe for Apple Chutney, but instead of apples, use 1kg (2lb) diced, fresh pineapple and 1kg (2lb) cooking pears. Do not include the centre core of the pineapple.

Plums in Alcohol

See section on Fruits in Alcohol, and the Rum Pot in particular.

Plum and Apple Chutney

Follow recipe for Apple Chutney, but use 1kg (2lb) apples and 1kg (2lb) plums.

Plum and Apple Jam

See Apple and Plum Jam.

Plum and Apple Sauce

Make up Plum and Apple Chutney, then continue as directed for Sauces.

Plum and Blackberry Jam

See Plum Jam. Use 1kg (2lb) cooking plums and ½kg (1lb) blackberries. Keep amounts of water and sugar the same.

Plum Chutney

Follow recipe for Apple Chutney, but instead of apples, use 2kg (4lb) stoned cooking plums.

Plum and Clementine Jam

See Plum Jam. For an unusual and fragrant flavour, allow the finely grated peel of 2 clementines to every 1½kg (3lb) fruit and add with the sugar.

Plum and Crab Apple Butter

See section on Fruit Cheeses and Butters.

Plum and Crab Apple Cheese

See section on Fruit Cheeses.
Use equal amounts of stoned plums and cut-up crab apples.

Plums, Dark Red, Bottled

Stalk plums then wash and dry. Treat exactly as Cherries, Red and Black, Bottled – see appropriate entry.

Plums, Dried

See Apples, Dried. Also read section on Drying. Choose dark red plums which are plump and perfectly ripe. Wash and gently wipe dry. Arrange plums on trays. Allow about 6 to 9 hours drying time if the process is continuous, or several days if the process is intermittent. The plums are ready when they are as wrinkled as prunes.

To prevent the skins from splitting, the oven temperature should be kept at 50°C (120°F) Gas ½, until the skins begin to wrinkle and then gradually increased to 66°C (150°F) Gas 2. This slightly higher temperature should then be maintained until drying is complete.

Plums, Frozen

Treat exactly as Greengages, Frozen – see appropriate entry. Dark plums freeze better than light ones.

Plum Jam

For a yield of 2¼kg (5lb) use:
1½kg (3lb) cooking plums (stoned for preference), 275ml (½pt) water and 1½kg (3lb) sugar. For instructions, see Jam section.

Plum and Peach Jam

See Plum Jam. Use 1kg (2lb) cooking plums and ½kg (1lb) slightly under-ripe and skinned peaches. To skin peaches, cover with boiling water and leave about 1 minute. Transfer to bowl of cold water. Drain. Remove skin. Cut up flesh with a stainless knife.

Plums, Pulped and Frozen

Treat exactly as Greengages, Pulped and Frozen – see appropriate entry.

Plum Sauce

Make up Plum Chutney, then continue as directed for Sauces.

Plums, Stewed and Frozen

Treat exactly as Fruit, Stewed and Frozen – see appropriate entry.

Plums, Stoned and Bottled

Halve and stone plums. Pack fruit into jars. Treat exactly as Blackberries, Bottled, but adjust methods as follows:

Method 1
Raise temperature to 82°C (180°F) and maintain ¼ hour.

Method 2
Same temperature as blackberries but maintain 20 minutes.

Method 3
Not recommended.

Method 4
Same as blackberries but process ½ to 2kg (1 to 4lb) for 50 to 60 minutes; 2¼ to 4½kg (5 to 10lb) for 65 to 80 minutes.

Method 5
Same process as blackberries but maintain pressure for 3 to 4 minutes.

For Methods 1 and 2, allow extra time for large-size jars as given at end of blackberry entry.

Plums, Sweet-Sour

Follow recipe for Pears, Sweet-Sour. To prepare plums, prick them all over to stop fruit from shrivelling, and simmer whole. Alternatively, halve plums and remove stones before simmering.

Potato Chips, Frozen

Cut peeled potatoes into even-sized chips then soak 1 hour in cold water. Drain and dry thoroughly. Fry in deep hot fat or oil until just tender but still uncoloured. Cool. Freeze by 'Free Flow' method described on page 29. Store in polythene bags or containers for up to six months. Chips should be fried from frozen state until golden in deep hot fat or oil.

Potatoes, Duchesse and Frozen

Prepare Duchesse potatoes as directed in your own recipe book and pipe on to lightly greased baking trays. Freeze by 'Free Flow' method described on page 29. When frozen solid, layer into containers with interleaving sheets between. Store up to six months.

Reheat and brown in hot oven before serving, once more placing rounds on lightly greased trays.

Potatoes, New and Frozen

Choose small, even-sized potatoes. Scrape and wash then par-boil in salted water. Drain. Freeze in polythene bags or containers. Store up to three months.

Note: The potatoes taste at their best if tossed in butter after draining and packed into bags or containers with a sprig of mint. They should be partially thawed and reheated in a covered casserole in a moderate oven.

Prunes in Alcohol

See section on Fruits in Alcohol, with special reference to Prunes in Armagnac.

Prune and Pear Chutney

Follow recipe for Apple Chutney but instead of apples, use ½kg (1lb) pitted prunes and 1½kg (3lb) cooking pears.

Prune and Pear Sauce

Make up Pear and Prune Chutney then continue as directed for Sauces.

Q

Quince Butter

See sections on Fruit Cheeses and Fruit Butters.

Quince Cheese

See Section on Fruit Cheeses.
Follow directions for Apple Cheese but simmer fruit in water with the addition of 1 level teaspoon citric acid and finely grated peel of 1 small lemon to every 1kg (2lb) fruit.

Quince Jam

For a 2¼kg (5lb) yield use:
1kg (2lb) quinces (peeled and cored weight), 1¼ litres (2pt) water, juice of 1 large lemon and 1½kg (3lb) sugar. Cut the quinces into small cubes then follow instructions for making as given under Jam section.

Quince Jelly

Follow recipe for Apple Jelly, but instead of apples, use 2kg (4lb) quinces and simmer in 2½ litres (4pt) water.

Note: The set will be better if the quinces are slightly under-ripe.

R

Raisin and Rhubarb Jam

See Rhubarb and Ginger Jam. Instead of ginger, add 125g (4oz) seedless raisins to the ingredients in pan before bringing to the boil. The finely grated peel of 1 large orange adds a distinctive flavour to the jam.

Raisins, Seedless

See section on Mincemeat.

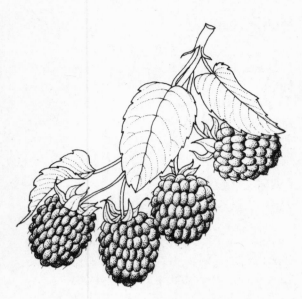

Allow 350g (12oz) sugar to every 575ml (1pt) strained fruit juice.

Raspberry Jam

For a 2¼kg (5lb) yield use:
1½kg (3lb) raspberries and 1½kg (3lb) sugar. Put berries into pan. Crush over medium heat until juice runs. Gently bring to boil. Add sugar. Stir until dissolved. Boil briskly until set. For further instructions, see Jam section.

Raspberry (Frozen) Jam

Read Freezer Jams in Jam section on page 54. For a yield of about 1½kg (3½lb) use:
550g (1¼lb) ripe raspberries, 2 tablespoons lemon juice, 1¼kg (2½lb) sugar, ½ bottle (125ml or 4 fl oz) liquid pectin.

Raspberry Jelly

Follow recipe for Apple Jelly but instead of apples, use 2kg (4lb) raspberries. Simmer fruit in only 6 tablespoons water, crushing it with a wooden spoon until it just begins to boil and bubble gently.

Raspberries, Pulped and Frozen

See section on Freezing with particular reference to Fruit Purées. Follow Method 1 using misshapen and uneven-sized berries. Freeze up to one year.

Raspberry and Redcurrant Jam

See Raspberry Jam. Use half raspberries, half redcurrants and 150ml (¼pt) water. Keep amount of sugar the same.

Raspberries in Alcohol

See section on Fruits in Alcohol.

Raspberries, Bottled

Carefully hull raspberries. Treat exactly as Blackberries, Bottled – see appropriate entry.

Raspberries, Frozen

Choose fully ripe fruit in prime condition. Freeze following either Method 1, 2 or 3, depending on personal requirements. Freeze up to one year.

Raspberry and Gooseberry Jam

See Raspberry Jam. Use half raspberries, half topped and tailed gooseberries and 150ml (¼pt) water. Keep amount of sugar the same.

Raspberry and Gooseberry Syrup

See section on Fruit Syrups.
Make up Methods 1 or 2, adding *no* water.

Raspberry and Redcurrant Jelly

Follow recipe for Apple Jelly but instead of apples, use 1kg (2lb) redcurrants and 1kg (2lb) raspberries.

Raspberry and Rhubarb Jam

For a 2¼kg (5lb) yield use:
1kg (2lb) raspberries, ½kg (1lb) rhubarb (trimmed weight) cut into 2½cm (1in) pieces, 5 tablespoons water and 1½kg (3lb) sugar. For instructions, see Jam section.

Raspberry and Strawberry Jam

See Raspberry Jam.
Use 1kg (2lb) raspberries and ½kg (1lb) sliced strawberries. Add no water but keep amount of sugar the same.

Raspberry Syrup

See section on Fruit Syrups.
Make by Methods 1 or 2, adding *no* water. Allow 350g (12oz) sugar to every 575ml (1pt) strained fruit juice.

Red and Blackcurrants, Bottled

Stalk currants. Treat exactly as Blackberries, Bottled – see appropriate entry.

Red Cabbage, Pickled

Shred head of 1 large red cabbage finely, discarding discoloured and fractured leaves and the hard centre stalk. Place layers of cabbage and kitchen salt in a large bowl. Cover. Leave 12 hours. Rinse thoroughly and drain. Pack fairly loosely into jars. Fill with cold spiced vinegar. Leave about one week before eating.

Note: Use up within one month of making because if left longer, the cabbage loses colour and crispness.

Redcurrant and Blackberry Jelly

Follow recipe for Apple Jelly, but instead of apples, use ½kg (1lb) blackberries and 1½kg (3lb) redcurrants.

Redcurrant and Blackcurrant Jam

See Blackcurrant Jam. Use half redcurrants and half blackcurrants. Keep amounts of water and sugar the same.

Redcurrants, Bottled

Stalk currants. Treat exactly as Blackberries, Bottled – see appropriate entry.

Redcurrants, Frozen

See Blackcurrants, Frozen.

Redcurrant Jelly

Follow recipe for Apple Jelly but instead of apples, use 2kg (4lb) redcurrants.

Redcurrant and Raspberry Jam

See Raspberry Jam. Use half raspberries, half redcurrants and 150ml (¼pt) water. Keep amount of sugar the same.

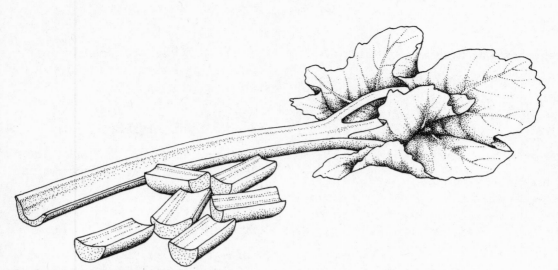

Redcurrant and Raspberry Jelly

Follow recipe for Apple Jelly, but instead of apples, use 1kg (2lb) redcurrants and 1kg (2lb) raspberries.

Redcurrants, Stewed and Frozen

See Blackcurrants, Stewed and Frozen.

Red Tomato Chutney

Follow recipe for Apple Chutney, but instead of apples, use 2¾kg (6lb) tomatoes. Heighten colour by adding 2 to 3 level tablespoons tubed or canned tomato purée with other ingredients. The dried fruits may be omitted if preferred. For a lighter-coloured chutney, use white sugar and distilled (colourless) vinegar. Tomatoes should be chopped but not minced.

Red Tomato and Green Pepper Chutney

Follow recipe for Apple Chutney, but instead of apples only, use 2¼kg (5lb) skinned tomatoes, 2 large, de-seeded green peppers, ½kg (1lb) apples and 1 tube (about 175g or 6oz) tomato purée to heighten colour.

Tomatoes should be chopped but not minced.

Red Tomato and Green Pepper Sauce

Make up Red Tomato and Green Pepper Chutney then continue as directed for Sauces.

Red, White and Blackcurrants, Bottled

Stalk all the currants. Treat exactly as Blackberries, Bottled – see appropriate entry.

Rhubarb and Apple Butter

See sections on Fruit Cheeses and Butters.

Rhubarb and Apple Cheese

See section on Fruit Cheeses.
Use equal amounts of apples and prepared rhubarb.

Rhubarb and Apple Chutney

Follow recipe for Apple Chutney, but instead of apples, use 1kg (2lb) apples and 1kg (2lb) rhubarb (trimmed weight).

Rhubarb and Apple Sauce

Make up Apple and Rhubarb Chutney then continue as directed for Sauces.

Rhubarb and Banana Chutney

Follow recipe for Apple Chutney but instead of apples, use 1kg (2lb) rhubarb (trimmed weight) and 1kg (2lb) bananas (peeled weight). If liked, substitute dried figs for dates.

Rhubarb, Bottled (for Dessert use)

Cut rhubarb into 2½cm (1in) lengths. Pack well down into jars then treat exactly as Blackberries, Bottled, but adjust methods as follows:

Method 1
Raise temperature to 82°C (180°F) and maintain ¼ hour.

Method 2
Same temperature as blackberries but maintain 10 minutes.

Method 3
Same temperature as blackberries but process ½ to 2kg (1 to 4lb) for 55 to 70 minutes; 2¼ to 4½kg (5 to 10lb) for 75 to 90 minutes.

Method 4
Same temperature as blackberries but process ½ to 2kg (1 to 4lb) for 40 to 50 minutes; 2¼ to 4½kg (5 to 10lb) for 55 to 70 minutes.

Method 5
Same process as for blackberries. Maintain pressure for 1 minute.
  For Methods 1 and 2, allow extra time for large-size jars as given at end of blackberry entry.

Rhubarb, Bottled (for Pies etc)

Trim rhubarb and cut into 2½cm (1in) lengths. Treat exactly as Blackberries, Bottled, so check appropriate entry.

Rhubarb and Fig Jam

See Fig and Apple Jam, but substitute rhubarb for apples.

Rhubarb and Ginger Jam

For a yield of 2¼kg (5lb) use:
1½kg (3lb) rhubarb (trimmed weight), juice of 3 large lemons, 25g (1oz) root ginger tapped lightly with a hammer to bruise it, and 1½kg (3lb) sugar. Put 2½cm (1in) lengths of rhubarb into large bowl with layers of sugar. Add lemon juice. Cover. Leave overnight. Tip into pan. Add ginger. Bring to boil. Boil rapidly until set. For further instructions, see Jam section.

Rhubarb and Lemon Jam

See Rhubarb and Ginger Jam. Instead of ginger, add the finely grated peel of 2 lemons to the ingredients in pan before bringing to the boil.

Rhubarb and Orange Chutney

Follow recipe for Apple Chutney but instead of apples, use 1½kg (3lb) rhubarb (trimmed weight) and ½kg (1lb) oranges which should be washed well, dried, left unpeeled and cubed. All pips should be discarded.

Note: This is a deliciously flavoured chutney and teams well with duck, goose, game and pork.

Rhubarb and Orange Sauce

Make up Orange and Rhubarb Chutney then continue as directed for Sauces.

Rhubarb and Raisin Jam

See Rhubarb and Ginger Jam.

Instead of ginger, add 125g (4oz) seedless raisins to the ingredients in pan before bringing to the boil. The finely grated peel of 1 large orange adds a distinctive flavour to the jam.

Rhubarb and Raspberry Jam

See Raspberry and Rhubarb Jam.

Rose Hip Jam

This is a cross between a fruit cheese and a jam and should be made from bright red, shining and plump hips. For a yield of approx 1kg (2lb):

Simmer ½kg (1lb) freshly gathered rose hips in 275ml (½pt) water until *very* soft. Rub through a nylon mesh sieve. To every ½kg (1lb) pulp, allow ½kg (1lb) sugar. Put both pulp and sugar into a preserving pan and simmer slowly, stirring frequently, until very thick. Pot and cover as directed in section on Fruit Cheeses and Butters.

Rose Hip Syrup

To retain as much vitamin C as possible, make in the following way:

Bring 1¾ litres (3pt) water to a brisk boil in an aluminium, stainless steel or unchipped enamel pan. Coarsely mince 1kg (2lb) ripe rose hips. Add to pan. Return quickly to boil. Remove pan from heat and leave to stand ¼ hour. Drip through scalded jelly bag. Transfer pulp from bag to saucepan. Add further ¾ litre (1½pt) water. Bring to boil. Leave to stand 10 minutes. Drip once more through jelly bag into first batch of rose hip juice. Pour into pan. Boil until no more than ¾ litre (1½pt) remains. Add ½kg (1lb) sugar, stir over low heat until dissolved then boil fairly briskly for 5 minutes. Pour syrup into bottles then process as directed in Fruit Syrup section.

Rose Petal Jam

Made regularly and eaten with great enthusiasm in Bulgaria and Romania, Rose Petal Jam is what I call a 'soft' preserve: very lightly set and therefore inclined to be runny. However, it is delicious and unusual, and worth making if you have an abundance of vivid, sweet-smelling red roses which are the only blooms of the rose family considered suitable for jam-making. The following amounts will make about ½kg (1lb):

Collect 225g (½lb) rose petals from flowers which have fully opened out. Tear gently into pieces and mix with 225g (8oz) caster sugar. Do this in a large bowl, cover and leave to stand for 48 hours. Heat 150ml (¼pt) water with another 225g (8oz) sugar, 2 teaspoons lemon juice and 2 teaspoons rose water (available from pharmacies). Stir until sugar dissolves. Bring briskly to the boil and continue to boil, uncovered, until a thick syrup has formed. (The syrup must not be allowed to colour.) Add petals and sugar and continue to cook gently for about 20 minutes or until jam is thick. Keep heat low and pan uncovered. Transfer to small pots and cover as described in Jam section.

Rowan Berry and Apple Jelly

Follow recipe for Apple Jelly but instead of

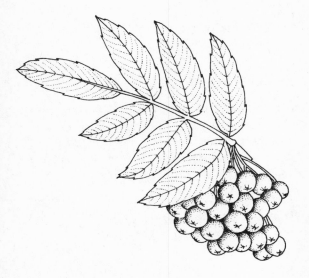

apples only, use 1kg (2lb) cooking apples and 1kg (2lb) rowan berries.

Note: Vivid red rowans are berries from the mountain ash tree and are popular in Scotland.

Rum Pot

See section on Fruits in Alcohol.

Runner Beans, Dried

See section on Drying.

Runner Beans, Salted

See section on Salting.

S

Sauerkraut

See section on Salting.

Seville Orange Marmalade

For a yield of 2¼kg (5lb) use:
¾kg (1½lb) Seville oranges, 1¾ litres (3pt) water, juice of 1 large lemon and 1½kg (3lb) sugar. Choose the most convenient method, for personal requirements, from Nos 1 to 4 in Marmalade section.

Seville Orange Marmalade with Rum

Follow recipe for Seville Orange Marmalade, stirring in 3 to 4 tablespoons dark rum as soon as the marmalade has reached setting point. Continue to boil a further 5 minutes. Pot and cover as directed in Marmalade section.

Shallots, Pickled

Follow recipe for Onions, Pickled.

Sloe and Apple Jelly

Follow recipe for Apple Jelly but instead of apples only, use 1kg (2lb) cooking apples and 1kg (2lb) sloes. Reduce water to 575ml (1pt). Continue as directed in Jelly section, allowing ½kg (1lb) sugar to every 575ml (1pt) juice.

Note: Sloes are dark, purplish-black berries with an acrid taste. They grow on blackthorn bushes and are used to flavour sloe gin.

Soft Fruit Syrup

See section on Fruit Syrups.
Make by Methods 1 or 2, using a selection of soft fruits to include strawberries, raspberries, gooseberries and loganberries. Add *no* water. Allow 350g (12oz) sugar to every 575ml (1pt) strained fruit juice.

'Solid Pack' Bottling

See section on Bottling, and entry on Apples bottled for dessert use.

Spinach, Frozen

Choose young, tender leaves and remove stalks. Wash leaves thoroughly. Blanch, a few at a time, for 2 minutes. Freeze in polythene bags or containers. Store up to one year.

Strawberries in Alcohol

See section on Fruits in Alcohol, and the Rum Pot in particular.

Strawberries, Bottled

See section on Bottling with particular reference to strawberries on page 12. Treat exactly as Cherries, Red and Black, Bottled, so check appropriate entry. Where jars have to be filled with hot syrup, pour off syrup from strawberries and heat in pan to required temperature. Otherwise use cold.

It is important to note that strawberries should *not* be bottled by Method 3 (slow oven). If bottled by Method 5 (pressure cooker), the pressure should be maintained for 3 to 4 minutes.

Strawberries, Frozen

Choose small to medium berries which are firm and just ripe; not over-ripe. Follow either Methods 1, 2 or 3, depending on personal requirements. Freeze up to one year.

Note: All strawberries become flabby when completely thawed, so eat while still partially frozen and just beginning to soften.

Strawberry and Gooseberry Jam

See Gooseberry Jam. Use half gooseberries and half strawberries. Reduce water to 150ml (¼pt). Keep sugar the same.

Strawberry and Gooseberry Jelly

Follow recipe for Apple Jelly but instead of apples, use 1kg (2lb) gooseberries and 1kg (2lb) strawberries.

Strawberry and Gooseberry Syrup

See section on Fruit Syrups. Make by Methods 1 or 2, adding *no* water. Allow 350g (12oz) sugar to every 575ml (1pt) strained fruit juice.

Strawberry Jam (1)

For a yield of 2¼kg (5lb) use:
1¾kg (3½lb) hulled strawberries, juice of 1 large lemon, 1½kg (3lb) sugar. For instructions, see Jam section, remembering to crush down strawberries and lemon juice in saucepan over low heat, and then boiling briskly until reduced by *half* before adding sugar.

Strawberry Jam (2)

For those who like whole strawberry jam, follow recipe for Strawberry Jam (1), but choose small fruit. Put all ingredients together in saucepan and stir gently until sugar dissolves. Afterwards boil for about 20 minutes. Remove from heat. Stir in 2 bottles (each 225ml or 8 fl oz) pectin. For potting and covering instructions, see Jam section.

Strawberry (Frozen) Jam

Read Freezer Jams in Jam section on page 54. For a yield of about 1½kg (3lb) use: 550g (1¼lb) ripe strawberries, 2 tablespoons lemon juice, 1kg (2lb) caster sugar, ½ bottle (4 fl oz or 125ml) liquid pectin.

Strawberries, Pulped and Frozen

See section on Freezing with particular reference to Fruit Purées. Follow Method 1, using misshapen and uneven-sized berries. Freeze up to one year.

Strawberry and Raspberry Jam

See Raspberry Jam. Use 1kg (2lb) raspberries and ½kg (1lb) sliced strawberries. Add no water but keep sugar the same.

Strawberry Syrup

See section on Fruit Syrups. Make by Methods 1 or 2, adding *no* water. Allow 350g (12oz) sugar to every 575ml (1pt) strained fruit juice.

Sultanas

See section on Mincemeat.

Summer Fruit Jam

For a yield of 2¼kg (5lb) use: 1½kg (3lb) mixed fruit to include diced rhubarb, gooseberries and strawberries. Cook in 150ml (¼pt) water. Add 1½kg (1lb) sugar. For instructions, see Jam section.

Swedes, Frozen

See section on Freezing. Freeze in purée form.

Sweetcorn, Frozen

See Corn on the Cob, Frozen.

Sweet Corn Kernels, Frozen

Blanch cobs as given under Corn on the Cob entry. Afterwards cut off kernels with a sharp knife. Freeze in polythene bags or containers.

Note: Kernels may be frozen with peas.

T

Three Fruit Jelly Marmalade

Follow recipe and method for Jelly Marmalade on page 65. Instead of Seville oranges, use 2 grapefruit, 2 lemons and 1 sweet orange to give total weight of 1kg (2lb).

Tomatoes, Frozen

Halve unpeeled tomatoes. With cut sides uppermost, fry lightly in butter or margarine. Transfer to trays, top with flakes of butter or margarine and freeze by 'Free

Flow' method described on page 29. When frozen solid, pack side by side in containers. Store up to one year. Partially thaw, then reheat under the grill.

Note: Tomato slices may be treated in the same way.

Tomato Purée, Frozen

Skin required number of tomatoes. Blend fruit until smooth in blender goblet. If liked, strain to remove seeds and heighten colour by whisking in tubed or canned tomato purée. Season with salt, pepper and sugar to taste. Pour into rigid containers, leaving 5cm (2in) headroom for expansion. Cover, seal and label as directed. Store up to one year. Thaw before using in cooked dishes.

Tomato Jam

For a yield of about 1¾kg (4lb), use:
1¼kg (2¼lb) skinned and chopped tomatoes, 1¼kg (2¼lb) sugar, finely grated peel of 1 large lemon, juice of 2½ large lemons, 175g (6oz) chopped stem ginger in syrup, 1 × 225ml bottle (8 fl oz) liquid pectin.

Put tomatoes into large bowl with sugar. Toss round. Leave to stand for 2 hours. Transfer to pan. Add rest of ingredients. Stir over low heat until sugar dissolves. Boil fairly briskly for ½ hour, stirring often. Re-

move from heat. Stir in pectin. Leave jam in pan until a skin forms on surface. Pot and cover as directed in Jam section.

Note: Although this jam forms a sugary and protective top layer, the jam underneath has a softish consistency. The flavour is distinctive and subtle and the colour most attractive.

Tomatoes, 'Solid Pack' Bottled

See section on Bottling and, in particular, blanched and cut-up tomatoes for 'solid pack' described on page 12. Choose most convenient method (excluding 3 or slow oven) and proceed as follows:

Method 1
Fill tomato-packed jars with cold brine. Fit on lids etc. Immerse jars in cold water. Raise temperature to 88°C (190°F) in 1½ hours. Maintain temperature 40 minutes.

Method 2
Fill tomato-packed jars with hot brine. Fit on lids etc. Immerse jars in lukewarm water (blood heat). Bring water to simmering point (88°C or 190°F) in ½ hour. Maintain jars at simmering temperature for 50 minutes.

Method 4
Stand tomato-packed jars on trays. Fill with boiling brine. Add rubber rings and lids but do not attach screw bands or clips. Put into oven preheated for ¼ hour to 150°C (300°F), Gas 2. Process ½ to 2kg (1 to 4lb) for 70 to 80 minutes; 2¼ to 4½kg (5 to 10lb) for 85 to 100 minutes.

Method 5
Fill tomato-packed jars with boiling brine. Fit on rubber bands, lids, screw bands or clips. Loosen screw bands by ¼ turn. Stand

1 or 2 jars in pressure cooker containing 2½cm (1in) boiling water. Cover. Heat till steam comes out of vent. Add 2½kg (5lb) weight. Bring up to pressure over period of 5 to 10 minutes. Maintain pressure for ¼ hour. Continue as directed on page 14 in Method 5.

For large jars bottled by Methods 1 and 2, allow extra time as follows: 1½ and 2kg (3 and 4lb), 10 minutes; 2¼ and 2¾kg (5 and 6lb), 20 minutes; 3¼ and 3¾kg (7 and 8lb), 30 minutes.

Tomatoes, Whole, Bottled

See section on Bottling and, in particular, method of preparing whole, unskinned small tomatoes as described on page 12. Choose most convenient method from 1 to 5 and proceed as follows:

Method 1
Fill jars with cold brine and other ingredients listed. Fit on lids etc. Immerse jars in cold water. Raise temperature to 88°C (190°F) in 1½ hours. Maintain temperature ½ hour.

Method 2
Fill tomato-packed jars with hot brine and other ingredients listed. Fit on lids etc. Immerse jars in lukewarm water (blood heat). Bring water to simmering point (88°C or 190°F) in ½ hour. Maintain jars at simmering temperature for 40 minutes.

Method 3
Stand tomato-packed jars on trays. Put into oven preheated for ¼ hour to 120°C (250°F), Gas ½. Process ½ to 2kg (1 to 4lb) for 80 to 100 minutes; 2¼ to 4½kg (5 to 10lb) for 105 to 125 minutes. Fill *after* processing with boiling brine. Attach rings, lids etc.

Method 4
Stand tomato-packed jars on trays. Fill with boiling brine. Add rubber rings and lids but *do not* attach screw bands or clips. Put into oven preheated for ¼ hour to 150°C (300°F), Gas 2. Process ½ to 2kg (1 to 4lb) for 60 to 70 minutes; 2¼ to 4½kg (5 to 10lb) for 75 to 90 minutes.

Method 5
Fill tomato-packed jars with boiling brine. Fit on rubber bands, lids, screw bands or clips. Loosen screw bands by ¼ turn. Stand 1 or 2 jars in pressure cooker containing 2½cm (1in) boiling water. Cover. Heat till steam comes out of vent. Add 2½kg (5lb) weight. Bring up to pressure over period of 5 to 10 minutes. Maintain pressure for 5 minutes. Continue as directed on page 14 in Method 5.

For large jars bottled by Methods 1 and 2, allow extra time as follows: 1½ and 2kg (3 and 4lb), 5 minutes; 2¼ and 2¾kg (5 and 6lb) 10 minutes; 3¼ and 3¾kg (7 and 8lb), 15 minutes.

Turnips, Frozen

See section on Freezing. Freeze in purée form.

V

Vegetable Purées, Frozen

See section on Freezing with particular reference to Vegetable Purées.

W

Walnuts, Pickled

Choose required number of walnuts, ensuring they are green and without shells. To test, prick walnuts with a needle. If easy to pierce, the shells have not yet formed. If there is resistance, it means shells have begun to build up from opposite the stalk ends. These walnuts are past their prime for pickling and others should be used instead.

Cover walnuts with brine and leave for 7 days. Drain. Cover with fresh brine. Leave a further 7 days. Drain. Spread out on trays. Leave to 1 to 2 days, exposed to the air, until the walnuts turn black. Pack into jars. Fill with hot spiced vinegar. Cover. Leave at least one month before eating.

Walnuts, Sweet-Sour

Follow recipe for Walnuts, Pickled. Pack walnuts into jars then cover with hot spiced vinegar boiled for 10 minutes with soft brown sugar. The basic proportion is $\frac{1}{2}$kg (1lb) sugar to every $1\frac{3}{4}$ litres (3pt) vinegar.

White Cabbage, Salted

See section on Salting.

Whortleberry and Apple Jam

See Apple and Bilberry Jam.

Whortleberry and Apple Jelly

This is identical to Bilberry and Apple Jelly – see appropriate entry.

Whortleberries, Bottled

Choose fruit in prime condition. Treat exactly as Blackberries, Bottled – see appropriate entry.

Whortleberries, Frozen

See section on Freezing. Follow Methods 2 or 3. Store up to one year.

Whortleberries, Stewed and Frozen

Treat exactly as Fruit, Stewed and Frozen – see appropriate entry.

Whortleberry Syrup

This is identical to Bilberry Syrup – see appropriate entry.